Under the Circumstances

A

WOMAN'S

GUIDE

TO A

SURRENDERED

HEART

JUDY HAMPTON

FOREWORD BY LUCI SWINDOLL

NAVPRESS

BRINGING TRUTH TO LIFE

P.O. Box 35001, Colorado Springs, Colorado 80935

OUR GUARANTEE TO YOU

We believe so strongly in the message of our books that we are making this quality guarantee to you. If for any reason you are disappointed with the content of this book, return the title page to us with your name and address and we will refund to you the list price of the book. To help us serve you better, please briefly describe why you were disappointed. Mail your refund request to: NavPress, P.O. Box 35002, Colorado Springs, CO 80935.

The Navigators is an international Christian organization. Our mission is to reach, disciple, and equip people to know Christ and to make Him known through successive generations. We envision multitudes of diverse people in the United States and every other nation who have a passionate love for Christ, live a lifestyle of sharing Christ's love, and multiply spiritual laborers among those without Christ.

NavPress is the publishing ministry of The Navigators. NavPress publications help believers learn biblical truth and apply what they learn to their lives and ministries. Our mission is to stimulate spiritual formation among our readers.

© 2001 by Judy Hampton
All rights reserved. No part of this publication may be reproduced in any form without written permission from NavPress, P.O. Box 35001, Colorado Springs, CO 80935. www.navpress.com
Library of Congress Catalog Card Number: 00-053720
ISBN 1-57683-227-9

Cover design by Dan Jamison
Cover photography by Bill Brooks / Masterfile
Creative Team: Nanci McAlister, Ken Gire, Pam Mellskog, Lori Mitchell, Amy Spencer, Glynese Northam

Some of the anecdotal illustrations in this book are true to life and are included with the permission of the persons involved. All other illustrations are composites of real situations, and any resemblance to people living or dead is coincidental.

Unless otherwise identified, all Scripture quotations in this publication are taken from the *New American Standard Bible* (NASB), © The Lockman Foundation 1960, 1962, 1963, 1968, 1971, 1972, 1973, 1975, 1977, 1995. Other versions used include: *The Message: New Testament with Psalms and Proverbs,* (MSG) by Eugene H. Peterson, copyright © 1993, 1994, 1995, used by permission of NavPress Publishing Group; the *Holy Bible: New International Version®* (NIV®). Copyright © 1973, 1978, 1984 by International Bible Society. Used by permission of Zondervan Publishing House. All rights reserved; the *Good News Bible Today's English Version* (TEV), copyright © American Bible Society 1966, 1971, 1976; and *The Living Bible* (TLB), copyright © 1971, used by permission of Tyndale House Publishers, Inc., Wheaton, IL 60189, all rights reserved.

Hampton, Judy, 1943 -
    Under the circumstances : a woman's guide to a surrendered heart / Judy Hampton
        p. cm.
    ISBN 1-57683-227-9 (pbk.)
    1. Hampton, Judy, 1943- 2. Christian biography--California. I. Title.
BR1725.H2343 A3 2001
277.3'0825'092--dc21
[B]   00-053720

Printed in the United States of America

1 2 3 4 5 6 7 8 9 10 / 06 05 04 03 02 01

FOR A FREE CATALOG OF
NAVPRESS BOOKS & BIBLE STUDIES,
CALL 1-800-366-7788 (USA)
OR 1-416-499-4615 (CANADA)

To my prince, Orvey,
who was changed by the King.

Next to Jesus, you are the most vital force in my life. Thank you for believing in my wildest dreams and my desire to tackle new horizons. You have rejoiced with me, encouraged me, and prayed for me like no one else. God took our broken lives and made them into something so beautiful, it's hard to comprehend. Watching you grow into such a passionate follower of Jesus Christ has blessed my life, our marriage, and the lives of our family. You model humility and integrity, and I am eternally grateful for you.

Contents

❧

Foreword

As I have had the good fortune to be friends with Judy Hampton for the past twenty-five years, I've noticed two characteristics that permeate her life: the transparent honesty of Judy and the constant faithfulness of God. I've known Judy when she was up and when she was down. I've seen her laugh and cry. I've held her hand when we've sung praises together and suffered with her when she wanted to give up and throw in the towel. But never have I known Judy to fake it in any way or to be anything other than who she really is . . . a truly genuine, wonderful, warm person.

By the same token, I've witnessed the provision of God over and over in Judy's life and that of her family, because He is faithful to His Word. And, in the circumstances of her life, she learned to take Him at His Word. She realized He could be trusted. God's faithfulness is a gift of His grace, not something earned because we behave ourselves. So even in the years Judy wasn't behaving herself, God was faithfully at work. She learned that.

This book is a reflection of blending honesty with faithfulness. As I read it, it was as though I was sitting with Judy on my sofa, laughing, talking, sharing our hearts . . . just like old times. She was hilariously funny and witty, as well as kind, thoughtful, and encouraging. Always honest. I could hear her voice as I read, see her face, and enjoy her thrill and excitement over knowing the Lord and telling me all the things He's done in her life—even those things He's doing today. She is that real . . . and this book is that transparent. You're going to love it!

Eugene Peterson's text from *The Message* in 1 Timothy 6:6 reads: "A devout life does bring wealth, but it's the rich simplicity of being yourself before God." Because Judy is herself before God, she enjoys a very wealthy life. It is full of joy and peace and humor and love and generosity. But it wasn't always that way. For years she lived in a dream world thinking wealth was found in a perfect marriage, home, children, and bank account. However, as those things failed to satisfy or materialize, God finally got Judy's attention and taught her that she was already a millionaire in Him.

I love being friends with Judy Hampton and seeing how God meets her in every phase of her life. This book is a tribute to the simplicity and beauty of being yourself.

— *Luci Swindoll*
author and speaker

Preface

Over the years I've been asked, "How ya doing, Judy?" My response? "Pretty good, under the circumstances." Yet few things have tripped me up in life more than being "under the circumstances." Why? Circumstances inevitably determined my joy and my peace. I allowed them to be my spiritual barometer. When life went my way, I was happy. However, when circumstances were less than perfect, I felt anger, fear, and even depression.

I mapped out a plan for my life from the time I was a child. This plan included attending college, marrying a terrific guy, experiencing a wedding like Cinderella's, living in the house of my dreams, having two children who made me look good, as well as having plenty of money, pleasure, and significance—all topped off with a glorious exit into heaven. My motto was "Thy will be done, as long as it's mine."

When I met Jesus, this life plan went up in smoke. After my conversion, I was a new woman ready to tell the world about Christ. However, I translated the abundant Christian life into the world's view of "the good life."

I am not proud that I spent so many years—even as a Christian—living under the circumstances in a victory/defeat mode. Yet it was "under the circumstances" where God got my attention. I finally realized that by changing my view of circumstances, I could change my response.

For instance, if I chose to view adverse circumstances with a victim mentality (a human viewpoint), my response would often involve fear and anger. However, understanding and believing that God is in control of all the circumstances in my life produces a totally different response.

How? First, God uses the circumstances in our lives so we can bring His light into a dark world. Second, He uses them to reveal areas in us that are not like Him, so that He might conform us into the image of His Son. It is through all the circumstances in our lives that He accomplishes His will. This is the divine viewpoint, and embracing it produces a response evidenced by peace and joy.

This change of viewpoint represented the most significant paradigm shift in my Christian walk. I was no longer trapped "under the circumstances." Jesus had set me free. Looking back, I see how He's used some pretty difficult circumstances to change me. And I see the way He's used my circumstances as a way to tell others about Him.

Are you struggling under the circumstances of life? Do you think that they must change in order for you to find happiness? If so, I believe you will find a new way of living in the pages of this book. It's a manuscript about a very slow learner, a very patient God, and a very wonderful freedom.

May you find the same freedom.

— *Judy Hampton*

Acknowledgments

❧

For me, writing a book seemed monumental. So I began, and it was monumental! But it was also extremely gratifying. Looking back over the years was an emotional journey. Yet seeing the faithfulness of God and His presence in all our circumstances blessed my heart. I am especially grateful for all the people who made this book possible and for their encouragement to write it.

My children, Joani and Doug (truly gifts from God):

You are the joy of my life. Thank you for years of love, enthusiasm, encouragement, laughter, and great friendship. I am extremely proud of both of you. I love watching God work in and through your lives.

My daughter-in-law and son-in-law, Cindy and Ed:

What a great and glorious God we know to bring two such outstanding people into my children's lives. You're the best!

My grandchildren, Brandon, Blake, Brittany, Eddy, and Lauren:

You have made growing old the most wonderful adventure. You bless my life in words I cannot describe.

My friends:

Thank you, Harriet, for leading me to Jesus Christ.

Thanks to all my "heart partners"—Joani, Judy, Kerry, Sunny, Cheryl, Diana, Diane, Susan, Marilyn, Luci, Ann, Carol, Sue, Bev, Evelyn, and Marcia. You are all women of prayer and genuine friends that care and encourage.

Thank you, Kay Werhas, for inviting me to be a part of your discipleship class. Your outstanding teaching of God's Word has kept my eyes on the goal for the prize of the upward call of God in Christ Jesus.

Thank you, Randy and Kerry Fitzpatrick, for generously giving me my first computer.

Thank you, Dick Shirk, for opening my eyes to the fine teaching on "circumstances." Thank you for allowing me to share this teaching and your nuggets of wisdom with others.

My valued publisher and team members:

NavPress, from the very first day I met you, you have made me feel welcomed and valued. Thank you for believing in my potential. Thank you, Nanci McAlister; your hands-on guidance and support have made all the difference in the world. Thank you, Ken Gire and Pam Mellskog, for your gifted editing and patience. Your hearts for God and His Word made a significant difference throughout the pages of this book and Bible study.

CHAPTER 1

Prince Charming in a Football Helmet

◈⌒

I couldn't *wait* to get inside my house. I'd kept my emotions inside during the long, uncomfortably hot bus ride home. But as I approached our weathered front door and inserted the key, the floodgates burst. I wept uncontrollably. "Why won't this stupid ol' door open?" I was desperate, wanting to hide and cry until every ounce of pain drowned in my tears. At last, the key turned, and I let myself in, grateful no one was home. No one, that is, except Rusty, our boxer, who greeted me at the door.

I dashed to my bedroom, threw myself on my bed, and wailed. Rusty jumped up and tried consoling me by licking my tear-soaked face and snuggling beside me, her warm fur pressed against my leg.

"Oh God, what am I going to do? Please, *please* don't let this be happening. This isn't what I had planned for my life," I pleaded.

That afternoon all my dreams and goals had been crushed. I had developed an unstoppable bloody nose at work, and my coworkers insisted on taking me to the hospital. Besides treating the minor emergency, the doctor discovered that my blood pressure was 180 over 80 and decided to conduct a more thorough examination. That's when he confirmed my suspicions—I was two months pregnant.

Seventeen years old, unmarried, and pregnant.

"What am I going to do? What am I going to do?" I screamed.

I couldn't fathom dealing with the responsibility. There had to be a way out. There must be a way out! My emotions then turned from panic to rage. I pulled on my hair and pounded my fists into the pillow yelling, "I don't deserve this!"

Every solution seemed insane. Back then in the sixties, abortions only happened in the shadowy back rooms of sleazy buildings or in filthy hospitals in foreign countries. I remembered our neighbor's daughter going that route a few months earlier. The thought sent chills through me. On top of that, I was broke! So I planned to leave New Mexico and stay with my aunt and uncle in Ohio for the next seven months. There I could secretly deliver the baby and give it up for adoption.

That's it, I decided. *That's what I'll do. I'll get my life back and go on as though none of this ever happened.*

By now I was emptying my room of every memento I'd collected since third grade. I bagged everything—a cheerleader outfit, swimming ribbons, autographed pictures of movie stars, teenage love letters, trinkets, and photo albums from happier days—and hauled it out to the backyard. Sobbing, I buried the memorabilia in the garbage bin. After all, if my carefree life was over, why keep any reminders of it?

Walking back to the house, I felt something of my alcoholic father's heartache for the first time. Plenty had gone awry in his life, too. For instance, before immigrating to the United States, he lived an impoverished childhood in Scotland. He lost his dad at an early age and suffered numerous other hardships growing up.

He was a loving and gifted man in so many ways, but because he chose to drown those memories in whiskey, his life went from bad to worse. All along, he refused to admit his addiction and eventually began drinking on the job. His drinking problem came to a head when I was fifteen: the local newspaper printed his picture and a notice that he'd been fired for this abuse.

Humiliation, depression, and despair consumed him and he

began drinking more than ever. Like me, he believed he could only escape the embarrassment by running. So within six months we left my quaint hometown and moved to a larger city for a fresh start. When the doctor confirmed my pregnancy that afternoon, I understood why he made us move, why he felt we had to leave.

But moving didn't solve his problems. Dad found another job in the city, but quickly lost it due to his drinking. Month after month, this scenario continued and we eventually fell into desperate financial straits. My mom, my brother, and I found meager jobs, but our combined salaries didn't cover the family expenses. Plus, Dad's drinking had escalated to the point where he'd pass out, sometimes injuring himself when he fell. I felt such pity for him. He was on a collision course, and no amount of pleading could convince him to seek help. I couldn't look up to him, so I looked elsewhere for a positive male figure.

During the first year in my new high school, I found it. I noticed a young man's picture on the cover of our school newspaper as well as in the city paper. Talk about a positive male figure. He was "Prince Charming in a Football Helmet." He was the star quarterback, sportsman of the year, an all-state wrestler, and a track star. He was extremely popular, an excellent student, and respected by his peers. I couldn't wait to meet him. Unfortunately, he was dating someone else.

Our senior year, as God ordained it, his locker happened to be right next to mine. Okay, I confess. I actually paid someone to switch lockers with me! Each time he came to his locker, I just happened to be at mine. We began flirting with each other. I always seemed to have problems opening my locker and, of course, needed his help. Finally, he asked me out. My response was silent hysteria, and I thought, *I did it! I did it! I got a date with the most popular fella on campus!* That afternoon I beelined home and barged in the back door.

"Mom! Mom! You'll never guess who asked me out!" I yelled.

"Who?" she asked, wondering if I'd lost my senses.

"Orvey! Orvey Hampton! Oh, Mom, he's adorable. Everyone at

school thinks he's dreamy. He's a great athlete, lots of fun, popular, and Mom, he asked me out. Can you believe it? *Me?* I mean, I am a big nobody at school, and he still asked me!"

Mom listened to me ramble on without saying a word. I figured she was impressed. Finally, she interrupted.

"Why on earth would a mother name her child Orvey?" she asked.

Good question. I'd never given it a thought, but I didn't care what his name was. He was the catch of the century, and he asked me out! I'd always silently sung that tune from *Cinderella,* "Someday my prince will come," and I was convinced Orvey Hampton fit the bill. It was the first ray of sunshine in a year. I was ecstatic and ran to my room to mentally replay his invitation. I tried on everything in my closet and eventually decided on the royal blue sweater with a matching skirt that Mom had given me for Christmas. I called several of my friends to see if they had some spectacular accessories I could borrow. Everyone was thrilled about my date with the prince.

It was months before I learned his full name: Orvey Euclid Hampton, Jr. His dad's name is Orvey Euclid Hampton, Sr. When I began dating Orvey Euclid Hampton, Jr., I thought it was a match made in heaven. I couldn't wait to get up every morning and go to school. When we weren't in classes, Orvey and I spent every waking moment together. I was so "in love" I couldn't eat. We attended all the dances together, wrote copious notes back and forth in class, talked for hours on end, participated in every school activity, double-dated with friends, and pined for each other as the school year passed.

Graduation was a month away, and we were planning our lives. Our blueprint looked like this: We would work the summer after graduation. Then Orvey would attend the University of New Mexico where he had received a full athletic scholarship. Several other colleges, including the Air Force Academy, had also offered scholarships. But this one provided the most benefits.

He wanted to study education. I, on the other hand, wanted to study law. He dreamed of playing professional football. I dreamed of making scads of money, getting married, having two children, and living happily ever after. Our plans sounded so dreamy, so perfect, so attainable — until graduation day arrived.

Of all days to desert us, Dad chose my graduation day. Worse yet, he left Mom a suicide note at the Western Union office that read: "Dorothy, I simply cannot stop drinking, and I can't support you, either. I left the car at the airport, and I'm going somewhere to take my life so you can get my insurance money. It's the only solution to my misery."

The letter devastated Mom. But the first thing I felt was intense anger. How could he be so selfish? Because of his actions, what should have been a joyful occasion turned sorrowful. No one felt up to attending my graduation, and Mom cried endlessly.

"What are we going to do?" she wailed. "I only have five dollars in my wallet. We are six months behind in our mortgage payments, and now they'll surely foreclose on us!" When my brother and I produced no answers, she used that five dollars to buy a bottle of bourbon.

In the end, my brother drove me to the high school. As I stood in line to receive my diploma, I wasn't appreciating my accomplishment or thinking about my future. Rather, I was praying — begging God to keep my dad from taking his life. But I wasn't even sure God was listening.

Until my dad disappeared, Orvey and I were confident about our plans. However, when two love-struck teenagers with enough hormones, enough time, and enough opportunity share a devastating crisis like mine, they often share something else. A few weeks after graduation, we made a decision that changed the course of our lives.

We had sex.

Six weeks after his graduation-day departure, Dad returned after he lost our car in a border town during an all-night drunk. Mom called me at a friend's house with the news and asked me to come home at once. When I arrived, a priest was standing at Dad's bedside.

"I can't remember where I've been or what I've been doing," he explained in a melancholy tone, "but when I ran out of money, I decided to come home. I borrowed a few bucks from a gas station owner and bought a bus ticket." He waited for sympathy. But how could I give him sympathy when he had ruined so much of my life?

I was relieved to see him, but I bitterly noted that he never *once* apologized. Nor did he offer any other explanation than the flimsy one he had just made. Instead, Dad milked the "victim" role to its limit. He whined about the rotten hand life had dealt him and about how pitiful our government was for not taking care of unemployed people like him. Even at rock bottom, he refused treatment for his drinking problem and argued that he could quit on his own. Of course, I'd heard it all a million times before.

I turned and left the room without a word. Sympathy? He may have gotten it from someone, but he sure didn't get any from me. As usual, I felt angry and disgusted. But that day, I was surprised by another feeling — gratitude.

"Thank You, God, for answering my prayers," I whispered to myself. I was so grateful Dad wasn't dead. Despite his dysfunction as a father, I was crazy about my dad. When he was sober, he was so loving and so much fun. When he wasn't sober, he was another man, one I hardly knew and couldn't trust.

Meanwhile, I gave Mom my meager paychecks to help support our family. My brother, then a college student, worked part-time for a shoe store and also contributed whatever money he could spare as he paid his way through school. Over the years, all this strain made us more determined than ever to build more meaningful lives for ourselves.

Until my fateful doctor's examination, it seemed possible. But my pregnancy, which I kept to myself for a month after the hospital visit, immediately changed my life. I felt sick much of the time, tired most of the time, and anxious all of the time. Even so, I had to keep working. After all, I had to put on a good front, and my family desperately needed the money.

Naturally, I told Orvey first. As we sat on the porch that hot August night, I felt nauseated about breaking the news, and my heart seemed ready to explode.

"I found out last month that I am expecting a baby," I finally blurted. "But I am planning to move to Ohio to live with my aunt and uncle. Then I'll give the baby up for adoption. I don't see any other solution. You have plans for college and football. I have plans, too. As soon as I have the baby, I want to continue my education. There isn't any way we can afford a baby. Not now."

After what seemed an eternity, Orvey finally spoke. In a tender, compassionate voice, he said, "Judy, this is my baby, too. I don't want someone else raising our child. Besides that, I love you. I want to make a life together. With you *and* our baby. We've talked about getting married. We'll just do it a little earlier, that's all. Sure, it isn't going to be easy, but we'll manage. Neither one of us is used to having money. We'll get by, somehow."

It wasn't my dream proposal. I had envisioned a splendid evening with an engagement party, music, flowers, and a beautiful diamond ring glittering on my finger. I was devastated at the idea of getting married so young. It was nothing like what I had read in the fairy tales of my childhood or the romance novels of my teenage years. I started to cry.

"I love you, too," I murmured. "I just never wanted our life together to begin like this!" We sat in silence, pensive over the hopelessness of our situation. Though it wouldn't be a Cinderella wedding, I knew getting married was the right thing for us to do. Yet the sun seemed to have slipped below the horizon of our dreams. The light had receded, and we were sitting in the shadows. Alone. All alone.

Within a week, we decided to tell our parents. We tried to think of a good time, but there wasn't any *good* time for news like this. When we walked into the living room, we found my dad napping in his old chair. Thank goodness he had been napping and not drinking.

"Daddy, Orvey and I need to talk to you," I said loudly. Stunned by our intrusion, his head jerked back. "What?" he blurted, trying to shake the sleep from his mind.

"Daddy, Orvey and I want to get married," I stated flatly.

"Oh really?" he calmly replied. "Are you pregnant?"

"Yes, Daddy, I am," I answered and began to cry. Before he could comment, Mom entered the room. She had heard the end of our conversation, and her response was not as kind.

"Well, is *this* the thanks we get for all we've done for you?" she snarled. "I hope you realize, young lady, that you've *ruined* my life! How could you *do* this to me?" she screamed. "I didn't raise a daughter to do something as disgusting as this. There's one thing you need to know, missy. Don't count on getting *anything* from us. You've made your bed, now sleep in it!" Then she stormed out of the room in tears.

That Dad was more understanding shouldn't have surprised me. After all, I had handed my paycheck to him for nearly two years, finished school, played nursemaid to both of them, and asked for nothing in return. They, on the other hand, hadn't contributed one red cent toward any of *my* needs. Throughout high school, I borrowed cars, clothes, and even a prom dress. And now, because I had committed the *unpardonable* sin, Mom walked out. My heart broke. I stood there in shock, convinced that her anger was not over me losing my virginity but over her losing my paycheck.

We left my house and drove in complete silence to Orvey's. His parents were spending a leisurely Friday night eating popcorn in front of the television. I felt such a sense of dread that I could barely sit on their sofa. I loved them so much. They were younger than my parents and more fun. Orvey's dad was a hard-working man who built and remodeled homes. His mom was a homemaker who built a home in her own way by raising a family.

"It sure is good to see you. What brings you out on a Friday night?" she asked pleasantly. As Orvey explained, they sat stunned at our story. Orvey was their pride and joy—the first Hampton to receive a college scholarship. Understandably, they dreamed their son would go on to make a good life for himself. He had just started college. Now all those dreams lay shattered on their living room floor.

"What are you going to do?" they asked. "What about college? What about football, your scholarship? How are you *ever* going to be able to provide for a family without giving that all up?" With each question I sank a little lower in the sofa.

"Judy and I have given this a lot of thought," Orvey said with a sigh. "She's going to continue working, and I'll continue going to college. Then we're going to get married this fall. The money that would normally go to my dorm fees will be enough to pay our rent. It will be rough going, but we know we can make it work."

Orvey was doing his best to convince them. And me. Tears filled the room, followed by a hush. After sitting for a while in somber silence, we finally left.

After that horrible, life-changing night, Orvey and I made plans to get married. We found a cheap apartment near the university and asked the priest who had visited my dad to marry us. We scheduled the date in November and invited only immediate family.

To keep our hastily planned wedding under wraps, we got the marriage license from another county so the news wouldn't appear in our local paper. Meanwhile, my mom sent announcements to our relatives in Canada, Michigan, and Ohio with the wedding dated the *previous* year. She was too ashamed to tell them the truth, so she tried to convince them we had been secretly married for some time.

Finally, we visited a jeweler and selected the cheapest rings we could find, which took less than ten minutes. What could have been a memorable outing was just another reminder of our lost dreams. The simple gold bands cost sixty-three dollars total. To pay for them, we opened a charge account and made five-dollar monthly installments.

On the morning before my wedding, my mom recited a quotation: "Happy is the bride the sun shines on." As I rode the bus to work, I felt angry. It was November, and although the sun was out, there was a chill in both the air and in my heart. Tears welled in my eyes. "The only thing that would make this bride happy is not having to get married at all," I pouted to myself.

After working a full day, and telling no one of my impending wedding, I took the bus home. I reluctantly dressed for the uneventful ceremony and drove to the church in silence with my family. Inside, the cluster of guests talked in hushed tones, as though they were attending the funeral of a disgraced relative, and the emptiness of the chapel echoed their voices.

Like most girls, I had dreamed of a storybook wedding ever since seeing *Cinderella*. I fantasized about the colors for my bridesmaids' dresses and visualized the flower cascades we would all carry. I pictured myself dressed in an exquisite gown with a majestic, twelve-foot train.

Turns out, we had no bridesmaids, no flowers, no music, and no photographer. My wedding dress was a homemade blue wool suit with a cheap carnation corsage pinned to the lapel. To get into the suit, I had to suck in my belly.

Finally, when my prince showed up, he was on crutches. Earlier that afternoon, he'd sprained his ankle in a scrimmage. Consequently, he took his vows while standing in pain, and I couldn't help thinking that this marriage was already starting out on the wrong foot.

After the ceremony, we dined at a small, inexpensive restaurant with red wallpaper and tired decorations intended to reflect an Old English theme. That was our wedding reception. People strained to share small talk and squeaked out "toasts" to the bride and groom. Dad wanted a highball. Mom just wanted to hide. She was afraid she might run into some friends and have to explain.

The moment we said, "I do," I was convinced our future would be as hopeless as my parents'. We were two teenagers with only ten dollars between us and a baby on the way. From a human viewpoint, judging by our circumstances alone, the future looked bleak.

CHAPTER 2

Perfect Marriages and Other Fairy Tales

⁂

$\mathcal{S}$ ince the beginning of time, we've been looking for perfect marriages. Actually, we've been looking for perfect *anything*—perfect home, perfect job, perfect health, perfect children, perfect income, perfect retirement. You name it. We've been looking for perfection ever since we lost it in the Garden of Eden.

We seem to miss perfect love most. That may explain why we are a nation of love addicts. Women seem especially love-struck as we spend millions of dollars each year on romance novels and line up for movies about unattainable bliss.

Consider *The Bridges of Madison County.* This movie centers on Francesca, a nurturing wife and mother who lives on a farm in Iowa. Despite her dedication to both family and farm, she continues feeling unappreciated by her husband. After years of this, a stranger named Robert comes along and sweeps her heart away. He treats her with kindness and romance. She soon feels cherished by him far more than by her husband. Like Orvey and me, they eventually sin by having sex outside of marriage. But it is "safe" sex. Why? Because nobody finds out. Nobody gets punished. And nobody seems to get hurt.

Sounds like an exciting romance, doesn't it? Or is it really just pure fantasy? Fantasies appeal to romantics, which is why I loved

Cinderella. Remember that wonderful "and they lived happily ever after" ending?

In off-screen marriages, though, "happily ever after" rarely happens—especially not overnight. Even the star-crossed Francesca and Robert, if they ever married, would soon realize that they fell in love with a myth. And myths have a way of crumbling under the weight of reality.

Over the long haul, Robert might not be so attentive, thoughtful, and romantic. Maybe he would start snoring. What would happen to this couple if he started leaving the toilet seat up and piling his dirty clothes on the floor? Francesca might one day stop fixing his favorite meals and start fixing only her favorites. She might gain weight and start wearing girdles during the day and frumpy flannel pajamas at night.

Because there is no such thing as the perfect mate, there is no such thing as a perfect marriage. Both are fairy tales. But when I got married, I believed in fairy tales. I thought the prince was responsible for Cinderella's happiness. Despite our rocky circumstances, I still dreamed of happily-ever-aftering in our very own castle. I was so naïve.

The day after our wedding, Orvey went to work. He wasn't supposed to work at all according to NCAA football scholarship rules, but we were desperate. So he covered local football games as a radio broadcast assistant and bused tables at a cafeteria in addition to receiving one hundred dollars a month from his scholarship. I earned two hundred dollars a month typing foreclosure notices at a mortgage company.

Still, we could only afford an apartment the size of a tool shed sparsely furnished with a hide-a-bed, desk, table, and two lamps. The kitchenette was so small the table had to be pulled down from the wall. And if the table were pulled down, no one could leave his or her seat. This kitchen set-up proved problematic during one of my first attempts at serving dinner.

Orvey didn't know that I had never cooked a full meal before, but I knew he loved Southern cooking—fried okra, collard greens, fried potatoes, red beans, and biscuits and gravy. After preparing the side dishes, I floured the chicken and cooked each side to a luscious, golden brown and served the meal.

Orvey was drooling. He happily took a gigantic bite out of the chicken, chewed, and suddenly stopped. He sat back from the table with a quizzical expression and then pulled a red vein out of his mouth. I was horrified. I had no idea chicken needed to be cooked *after* it was browned. I thought browned meant done! But the table was down, so we were stuck eating medium-rare chicken.

Besides being small, our one-room dump had no ambiance. Not one picture hung on the walls, and the biggest accessories were the cockroaches. I'd never seen so many in my life. Some were big enough to saddle up and ride. Plus, we always heard our neighbors when they argued. It never occurred to me that they could hear *us* arguing until they knocked on the wall during one of our less blissful moments.

The apartment added to my depression, as did Orvey's schedule. He worked nights while I sat home alone reading. There wasn't much to do and certainly not much to clean! I worked during the day, spent evenings alone, and on the weekends I would drive to my parents' home to do laundry. The month before our son's birth, I quit my job and slept most of the day. Sleeping wasn't alcohol, but it had the same effect.

When our son arrived, I felt a surprising sense of awe. What a precious, little miracle Douglas David was. Although he wasn't planned, I thanked God for him. He was beautiful, and our entire family loved him immediately.

Yet when we left the hospital in our decrepit '49 Ford, I was so embarrassed. I was sure the nurses thought to themselves, "Look at this pathetic young couple. Can they even provide for the child?"

I wondered myself. Taking responsibility for our baby frightened me. He was so helpless, and I had no idea how I was going to care for him. The doctor gave us a list of things we needed to buy before we went home, but we didn't stop because we had no money.

The first few days of parenting were a nightmare. I tried to nurse, but all the baby did was cry. Orvey insisted he was spoiled. Turns out he was famished because my milk wasn't satisfying him. So we had to borrow money from my mom to buy formula. During this time, our nerves were on edge, and we argued constantly. In desperation, I phoned for help.

"Mom, Doug is just crying and crying!" I explained. "I fed him, changed his diaper, rocked him, and walked him. I don't know anything else to do." As I cried, Mom said she didn't know what to say.

"I can't remember what I did when you kids were babies," she confessed. "That seems like a hundred years ago!" Luckily, Doug finally quit crying, and in a few weeks I felt more confident caring for him.

That progression relieved some of my stress, as did moving into a larger apartment in June. It was only a one-bedroom, but it seemed *huge* in comparison. Doug slept in our bedroom in a used crib a friend had given us. And with the last few dollars in our savings account, we bought a picture for the living room. This place was more like home.

That summer Orvey got a construction job that raised our standard of living a little more. While we had scrimped to buy our first television, we were married two years before we could afford the luxury of a telephone. Even so, our circumstances were definitely looking up. But I continued complaining about our finances, which filled our home with tension—even after I took a job later that summer that doubled my previous salary.

Meanwhile, Orvey poured himself into college and football for the next three years. His games were the brightest spot in our lives. He was an outstanding player, as well as an honor student. I loved it when he completed a pass or ran for a touchdown. During those years, the University of New Mexico team reigned as conference champion. Since childhood, Orvey had dreamed of the day he would become a professional football player. It looked like he was on his way. As for me,

I dreamed of the day I could afford to buy a decent dress.

We both worked long and hard to realize our dreams and keep our family afloat. At one point, the two of us held five different low-paying jobs. Evenings, we cleaned doctors' offices. Days, I sold Avon and worked office jobs. Weekends, Orvey bused tables and picked up odd jobs. We were *driven* to reach our goals.

"Whatever you do," I frequently reminded, "get that college degree so we can have some kind of life!"

In the 1960s we believed a college education was the ticket to the kind of financially secure, happy life we wanted. Since the first grade, our family and our teachers had told us that a degree guaranteed freedom from poverty and paved the pathway to success. After graduation, we expected great job offers to start pouring in. Because I believed all our problems were circumstantial, I just as fervently believed that they would all disappear the day Orvey landed a good job.

As graduation drew closer, the professional football career opportunity became less and less likely. Orvey got tryout invitations, but no offers materialized and he became depressed. With my usual compassion, I would make cutting cracks. "Well, have you noticed that I've *never* been able to realize any of my dreams? I've been too busy working at dead-end jobs to support you," I jabbed. "Just get a *job!* I am sick to death of being poor and struggling for everything."

Our communication deteriorated to silence. When we did talk, it was to criticize each other. Yet I continued holding him responsible for all my needs, both financial and emotional.

At this time, Orvey was working part-time at the university golf course and thoroughly enjoying the perk of playing free rounds. But when he came home, I made his life miserable. He returned the favor by leaving the parenting to me. I, in turn, seethed with resentment toward him. Small wonder he never wanted to come home.

To make matters worse, I needed major surgery. Shortly after I recovered, Orvey's mother was admitted to the hospital to recover from an emotional breakdown. Orvey's parents had moved from New Mexico to Oklahoma, and he immediately flew there to be by her side.

Because she was heavily medicated, she didn't recognize Orvey, and it broke his heart. Consequently, he returned home in an even deeper depression and secretly decided to drop out of college—though graduation was in sight. Life's unfulfilled expectations had devastated him.

A few weeks later, I came home from work with my arms full of presents for Doug's fourth birthday party. As I put the packages down, I noticed a handwritten note from Orvey on the table: "Judy, I have to get away. I haven't been attending college for quite some time, and I didn't know how to break the news. I need to get away for a while so I can sort out my life. I know I have been a miserable husband and have let you down, but I am very confused right now. I'm devastated over my mom. I love you. I'll call soon and let you know where I am living. Love, Orvey."

As I read the letter, I felt the blood drain from my head. I came close to passing out. Oppression filled the room like fog. For several minutes, I gazed out our kitchen window, tears streaming down my face. *Why bother trying to make this marriage work?* I thought. *I am so worn out with the constant disappointments. Isn't there anyone who wants to take care of me?* I muttered some choice, ugly words and threw the presents across the room.

My responsibilities brought me back to reality. We had a son in nursery school, and it was past time to pick him up. I phoned my dearest friend, Julie, and she promised to come and comfort me. Truth is, no one but a few friends even cared. I kept thinking of my mom's words: "You've made your bed, now sleep in it."

Now I would sleep alone.

During the short drive to Doug's school, anger oozed from every pore. *What about me? What about the sacrifices I've made? Why can't I run away?* I was filled with so much rage it was a miracle I didn't wreck the car. *Is this what men do when life gets hard?* Feelings about my dad running out on our family came flooding back to me.

Then, a few weeks after the separation, I learned I was pregnant. *Oh great! How much worse can life get? What am I going to do? How can I support two children on my salary?* History seemed to be repeating itself. "Tell me this isn't happening to me *again!*" I wailed.

The questions turned into exclamation marks. And the anxiety turned into depression. From a human viewpoint, life offered little hope. The weight of my circumstances seemed unbearable. I worked. I cried. I slept. All the while, I told no one.

After a long day at work, I would pick up my son from nursery school and head home to an empty apartment. I'd make a meager dinner for him, bathe him, read him a story, and tuck him into bed. He was content with my explanation that Daddy was working away for a while.

A great weariness settled on me. All I could do was put one foot in front of the other. Those feet led me to the living room where I would sit for hours and just cry. There on the couch, I thought a lot about my childhood. And I thought a lot about God.

The church I grew up in was beautiful. It had a rustic stone exterior and a majestic steeple. The services were traditional and included lots of liturgy. I loved it! Every Sunday, my childhood friend, Bunnie, and I asked our parents to drive us to church. There I memorized pages of prayers from a prayer book and faithfully quoted the creeds. I earned pins and crosses for good deeds and faithful works. I even gave up chocolate for Lent.

As I grew older, though, I invented my own brand of religion. I genuinely had a heart to know God, but I figured my relationship with Him was dependent on my measuring up. From a very young age, I promised Him I would be a good, moral person and not commit any of the Big Ten sins. I would live a good life in exchange for His blessing my life. That seemed fair.

When I got pregnant out of wedlock, I figured that I had

committed the *unpardonable sin*—that God was through with me. After I married Orvey, I still attended church, but only occasionally and obligatorily, because I got nothing out of it. Still I knew there was something missing in my life, but I had no idea what. I continued carrying my burdens, thinking that was part of my "punishment." I didn't know then that God is never finished with any of us, no matter what we've done. And I didn't know that even in these dark hours, He was drawing me to Himself.

In my loneliness and pain, I cried out to Him: "God, please help me or let me *die!*" This was my common prayer! I really didn't want to die. I just wasn't sure I could go on any longer. When I ran out of money and hope, Doug and I moved in with my parents.

Considering my circumstances, I was relieved when they took us in. But my father's attitude wounded me. He insisted that I pay for half of all the expenses incurred and insinuated that everything would be better if I lost the baby.

Meanwhile, Orvey lived in another state. I knew his address, but had little contact with him and no financial support. My parents encouraged me to divorce him. After calling an attorney, I wrote Orvey a letter notifying him of my change of address, my pregnancy, and my plans to file for divorce.

Yet I found myself praying every night for Orvey's safety. This sudden burst of spirituality surprised me. I still didn't know if God even heard my prayers, but I had a strong urge to keep praying. Then one evening the phone rang. It was Orvey. It was the first time he'd called in over a month. And my sudden burst of spirituality was overcome by a greater burst of carnality.

"What do you want *now?*" I asked coldly.

"Please let me come home," he begged. "I have made the biggest mess out of my life, and I've hurt you *so* much. I'm sorry, Judy. I want a second chance. I *need* a second chance. I want to be a good father for my children and a good husband to you. I want to restore our marriage."

I listened while gritting my teeth. As he talked, I wondered why I should believe him. After all, he had dumped me, humiliated me. This time was the last time. I was *determined* not to cave in to his persuasive ways. I'd had it with Orvey Euclid Hampton, Jr. I had put up with enough pain for a lifetime.

"Divorce is the only solution to this miserable marriage," I said. "No way am I ever going to find happiness married to a man I can't depend on. Staying with you, Orvey Hampton, is like a ticket to misery." And I slammed down the receiver.

His letters arrived daily, filled with ideas about what had happened to our lives. In those letters he shared his innermost thoughts and dreams, something he'd *never* done. Because I had been so critical, he probably hadn't felt safe sharing his feelings.

"I didn't leave *you*, Judy," he wrote. "I just had to escape from my life. I was desperate, depressed, and filled with disappointment. It seemed like the only viable solution. Everything in my life had failed to live up to my expectations and dreams, so I ran." Each letter was filled with adoration, resolve to "turn over a new leaf," and pleas to give him *one* more chance.

I knew I loved him, that I'd always loved him. But could I *trust* him? Could we ever put the past behind us? Could he ever become the husband I needed? That was the real question. It never occurred to me that I could be at least partly responsible for our messy marriage. I was angry, opinionated, and self-willed. A part of me wanted our marriage to work, especially for the children. But a voice whispered to me saying, "Judy, you deserve a better man than this. The world is full of great men. Why don't you dump this guy and get on with your life?"

Some days that voice sounded *so* convincing. So I resolved to stay strong and not open myself up to more pain — despite Orvey's sweet talk. However, I eventually gave in and my parents couldn't believe it.

"You did *what?*" Mom asked when I told her the news.

"I know, I know," I sighed. "But he sounds so sincere."

When Orvey came home, Mom and Dad reluctantly allowed him to move in so he could start looking for a job immediately. A month later, he started working as a dispatcher with a trucking firm and we found a large, two-bedroom apartment. By now, I had quit work to prepare for the birth of our second child.

Though our circumstances had drastically improved in the last couple of months, I feared that Orvey would bail again. I would wake in the middle of the night from nightmares generated by those fears. My heart would pound, and my skin would be covered in cold sweat. I was always aware that I could be a single mom at a moment's notice. I walked on eggshells, determined to please him any way I could. I wanted him to be happy and to love me. But *trust* him? I didn't think trust was possible.

Soon our beautiful daughter, Joani, arrived, and Orvey doted over this pink little bundle of joy night and day. Two months later, we moved from our apartment to a cute little house, and that's when we began putting the pieces of our broken lives back together. Part of that process involved going to church. I always coveted the "All-American-Family" image, and being in a nice home in a nice neighborhood rekindled my desire to attend.

"Church is just what we need," I nagged. "Let's start going, Orvey. Our *children* need to be in church." Orvey relented, but our attendance was infrequent. At Christmas and Easter we dressed in our Sunday best, piled the kids in the car, and headed off to the prettiest church we could find. There we heard skillfully prepared messages, but they sounded stale. Nonetheless, the music touched me, and somehow I left with a renewed sense of hope. But the effort to get to church continued to outweigh my need to be there.

A few months later Orvey got a nice promotion into sales. In that routine, though, he grew restless. To cure it, he joined a bowling league with the guys from work, played golf on the weekends, stayed out late some evenings playing cards, and announced his desire to finish his degree in night school. His life seemed full and satisfying. Mine seemed just the opposite. Home alone again, I decided to get a part-time job and make some mad money.

"When I am mad, I'll at least have money," I justified. I needed *something* to fill my emptiness. By now, our children were ages two and six. They were wonderful kids, and there was plenty to keep me busy, but it still wasn't enough. I needed something else. What, I didn't know. I only knew the craving hunger from the emptiness inside.

I found a part-time job, but I also found that the workplace had changed a lot in the past two years. On television talk shows and in talk around the water cooler, I began hearing a new philosophy. It sounded inviting, and it went something like this: "Men are the reason women are so miserable! They have used and abused women down through the ages. They've suppressed us, oppressed us, and now it's time to take back our rights! Men have dominated women long enough. It's time to take control. Why should women live in misery and make all the sacrifices?"

This new philosophy coincided with the whisper I'd heard a few years back. It was appealing. I'd been looking for someone to blame for my misery, and finally I had found him: Orvey Euclid Hampton, Jr. I had suspected it all along.

Hooray! I thought. *Look out, world. Whatever it takes—a better job, a better husband, a better life—I'm going to find happiness.* From a human viewpoint, I was merely taking back what I felt was rightfully mine—my life.

CHAPTER 3

The Visit

❧

The perfect man. The perfect marriage. They had to be out there somewhere, because they sure weren't here. *Out there, somewhere,* I mused. The ringing phone interrupted my daydream. It was my old friend Harriet Byrd announcing she was stopping by in thirty minutes to visit. The second I hung up, I began throwing things in closets, fluffing up pillows, setting out coffee cups, and grabbing Joani and Doug's faces with a damp washcloth.

As I was doing this aerobic housecleaning, Harriet's words echoed in my mind: "I just want to come by for a quick visit and an update on how things are going. I haven't seen your kids in ages, but I don't want you to go to any trouble."

Trouble? Harriet? Bless her heart. She'd been so faithful in listening to my constant stream of complaints! Small wonder she hadn't checked me off months ago, even though we hit it off the moment we met through our husbands when they played college sports together. And frantic as I was, dashing around my cluttered house, I looked forward to her visit. She always had such a calming effect on my terminally chaotic life. As soon as the aroma of the freshly brewed coffee filled our house, I heard her knock.

"Hi there!" I piped. "It's so good to see you, Harriet. Where's Tommy? Didn't you bring him with?"

"He's at his grandma's house taking a nap, and I didn't have the heart to wake him," she explained while stepping inside. "Anyway, this will give us a better chance to visit."

I plunked my kids down in front of the television and bribed them to stay put. Then Harriet and I headed to the kitchen, where I poured coffee and piled a plate of homemade cookies. We sat at the dining room table, sipped away, and started chatting. After the usual pleasantries, our conversation turned to more urgent matters, like my marriage, which happened to be in shambles.

"Oh, Harriet, I don't think Orvey loves me," I sobbed. "He works nonstop, stays out late bowling or playing cards. He's finishing his degree one night a week, and he goes golfing on the weekends. He seldom does what he says he's going to do, let alone anything I tell him to do. He's inattentive, and I simply don't trust him." My lips trembled as I spoke, and tears spilled from my eyes. "I simply can't change the man, and I am worn out trying. The thought of living the rest of my life like the past seven years sends chills down my spine." I took a deep breath and announced, "I'm considering divorce."

"Be honest, Harriet. Don't I *deserve* more out of life than an ungrateful, selfish husband who expects me to raise these children and do all the work? What about *me?* Don't I *deserve* someone who will love me and appreciate me and help me? To be frank, Harriet, I'm exhausted. From the day I got pregnant, my life has gone downhill. So far, nothing in life has lived up to my expectations, and I am sick of trying."

I continued, explaining how I thought my happiness was just a man away. He had to be out there somewhere. All I had to do was find him.

Harriet sat in silence. I had just dumped another load of complaints on her, but not once did she sigh, moan, or gasp. And not once did she interrupt. I later learned she didn't interrupt because she was paralyzed with fear over what she was about to share.

Finally, I took a breath. At that moment Harriet pulled out a little yellow booklet and, with all the courage of a soldier going into battle, began sharing the gospel of Jesus Christ.

"Judy, I have something to talk with you about that could be the answer to all your problems," she started. With the word "answer," she had my attention. "This booklet explains why you are experiencing such disillusionment," she continued. "Would it be all right if we read it together?"

"Sure!" I quickly replied. I figured she was going to tell me about a new method on how to change my *husband* or find a new one! Instead, Harriet opened *The Four Spiritual Laws* tract and began sharing about Jesus Christ.

"God loves you, and He has a wonderful plan for your life. So why is it that most people are not experiencing the abundant life?" she asked.

"I dunno," I replied. I just figured I needed to change my circumstances.

"Because man is sinful and separated from God," she answered.

Well, it's not every day a friend comes over for coffee and calls you a sinner. I'd grown up in church and had promised God I'd be a good person. But I felt I'd committed the unpardonable sin by having sex before marriage and getting pregnant. I figured it was too late. I had dropped my end of the deal.

Harriet continued reading the booklet and quoting Bible verses I'd never heard before like "All have sinned and fall short of the glory of God" (Romans 3:23). The booklet also pointed out that man had been created to have fellowship with God, but because of his stubborn self-will, he went his own way, and fellowship with God was broken. This self-will is characterized by active rebellion or passive indifference, and is evidence of what the Bible calls "sin."

By now Harriet had my *full* attention. I grew up in church, but if the pastor had been preaching *this* from the pulpit, I missed it—maybe because much of the time Bunnie and I were too busy checking out the new hairdos or fidgeting in the pews.

Harriet continued paging through the pamphlet to explain that "the wages of sin is death, but the free gift of God is eternal life in Christ Jesus our Lord" (Romans 6:23). I listened as she told me that I could experience a new beginning, a new birth, if I would just believe that Christ died on the cross for me!

"Harriet, I've never heard any of this," I confessed. "Where has all this stuff been? I have always loved God and considered myself a religious person. I have attendance pins to prove it. When I got pregnant, though, I felt God was finished with me. I didn't know that Jesus Christ died for my sins so I could be forgiven. Now you are telling me that *everyone* has sinned?"

"We must individually receive Jesus as our Savior and Lord before we can experience God's forgiveness, His love, and His plan for our lives," she shared. Then she read the verse, "Behold, I stand at the door and knock; if anyone hears My voice and opens the door, I will come in to him" (Revelation 3:20). When we reached the end of the booklet, Harriet explained another concept I'd never considered.

"First of all, the Bible says no one is righteous, Judy. Sin is sin," she stated. "But there are no unforgivable ones. Not if you know Christ. But knowing Christ isn't believing *about* Him. It's believing *in* Him. And that involves turning from sin and inviting Him into your life, asking Him to forgive your sins, and giving Him first place in your heart so He can make you into the person He wants you to be."

By now, a different kind of tears cascaded down my cheeks—spiritual tears. Tears that were drawing me into the presence of a *king*. Tears of hope. Tears of relief. Tears of cleansing. I couldn't believe what she was telling me. Answers to my questions? A new beginning for my past mistakes? Forgiveness for my sin? Love? Joy? Peace? Hope? I wanted to meet this God who had created me and who could make sense out of the miserable life I was experiencing.

"Harriet, I want to pray that prayer," I said quietly. "I want to pray it right now."

Harriet slowly read the prayer from the booklet. I repeated it with her. Although my children were in the next room playing, a holy hush fell on our dining table. It was as though we'd been ushered into God's throne room. I confessed my sins, made a choice to turn from them, and asked Him to forgive me. I thanked Him for dying for my sins and for giving me the gift of eternal life. On that day in October 1968, in a tiny kitchen, in a small house, in a modest neighborhood, on an ordinary street, I met Jesus, the King of Kings Himself. Who could forget a day like that?

When I finished the prayer, Harriet shared hers.

"Lord, thank You for saving Judy's soul," she began. "Thank You that there are *no* unforgivable sins, because You died for *all* our sins. Father, I pray Judy will let You change her life and give her the peace and purpose she's been searching for." It was so comforting to listen to her pray. It was the very first time in my life someone had actually prayed for *me*. She also asked the Lord to restore my broken marriage.

Immediately after our prayers, I felt different. It was hard to understand, even harder to express. How can you express a feeling you've *never* experienced? It was as though someone had emptied my heart of all its fear, all its anger, all its purposelessness, and replaced it with a peace I had never known. I had been born into the family of God. I wanted to laugh and cry at the same time.

"Harriet, thank you so much," I said as we hugged and wept. Little did I know that a choir of angels was rejoicing in heaven, while on earth a group of Christians I'd never met was praying.

That night when Orvey got home, I recounted the afternoon's events. "Honey, you'll *never* believe what happened," I said joyfully. "This is the greatest day of my life. Harriet Byrd came over to visit, and she shared a little booklet that clearly explained the gospel, and I invited Jesus to come into my life. I have become a Christian!"

Orvey's response was less than enthusiastic. "Judy," he said, "I did that when I was twelve years old at the Pioneer Baptist Church in Oklahoma City."

"Oh really?" I asked sarcastically. "You could have fooled me all these years, buddy! You bum! You mean you've known the answer to all of life and you've never once shared it with me?"

He didn't answer. I could tell by the look on his face that I'd hit a sore spot. He was embarrassed, and my remarks that night didn't open the door to any sweet celebration.

At the time I didn't understand that when we invite Christ into our lives, He promises He will *never* leave us or forsake us (see Matthew 28:20; Hebrews 13:5). Orvey had made that invitation as a young boy. Then he moved away from Oklahoma City and got sidetracked as a teenager. Like many, he thought he could find happiness living independent from God—at least until a crisis came along. As a result, he put his relationship with the Lord on hold. The longer he lived away from Christ, the harder his heart grew, and the more his circumstances controlled him.

Despite his cynicism, Orvey noticed the change in me. "Your *face* is different!" he remarked. It was true. I'd had a divine face-lift. I'd also changed the way I treated him and our children. He noticed that, too.

It was what the apostle Paul wrote about in 2 Corinthians 5:17: "Therefore if any man is in Christ, he is a new creature; the old things passed away; behold, new things have come." My life was being transformed. My priorities were changing, and it had nothing to do with me. It was Christ *in me,* the hope of glory.

Soon after my conversion, Orvey received another promotion that involved relocating to El Paso, Texas. Just the thought of moving from family and friends struck *terror* in me, terror I hadn't experienced since before I met Jesus. I still worried that our marriage wouldn't make it, and I didn't want to be far from family. After all, who wants to be a single mom stranded in west Texas?

One evening after the children were asleep, I decided to share my fears with Orvey. I had no idea what his response would be, and my heart pounded.

"Orvey, I am really excited about the job opportunity in Texas," I began. "You've worked hard and deserve the promotion. But your late hours, your withdrawal, and your silence are driving us further apart. I am terrified about moving 350 miles away, not knowing where I stand with you." I trembled as I spoke. "Maybe you'd rather move by yourself and begin a new life without me and the children. I know how unhappy you are, how restless. . . ."

CHAPTER 4

Beyond the Altar

Orvey interrupted to assure me of his love and commitment to us. I still felt insecure, but started packing anyway. He moved before us, and we planned on joining him as soon as Doug finished first grade. During that interim, Orvey came home every other weekend. But it wasn't enough to alleviate my worries.

"I'm scared," I shared. "Just plain scared. I've never moved from my home town except for when I was a kid."

Orvey assured me that the move would be exciting, that coworkers had already helped steer him toward some great housing prospects. True to his word, he rented the biggest home we had ever occupied, and it was in an established neighborhood with excellent schools. He spent evenings painting and preparing for our arrival.

Being a woman, I wondered what a man's idea of a lovely home was. For instance, I remembered my brother telling my sister-in-law that he had found an apartment in Norfolk, Virginia, with "modern" furnishings that she would love. Upon arriving, she realized he must have thought "modern" meant "brand-new." The new furniture was actually Early American.

Regardless of my lingering doubts, moving day arrived, and we bid farewell to our "roots" in New Mexico. Good-bye to comfort zones, good-bye to our families, and good-bye to our friends.

As my parents stood on their driveway, waving, tears streamed down their faces. They streamed down mine, too. God had healed many wounds over the months, and we'd grown to love and depend on them more. Our car was bursting at the seams with two children, a Schnauzer, and stuff we didn't think we could live without for a few days. We slowly made our way down the familiar street, towing my little red car behind. It was a new chapter in our lives. But both of us were apprehensive about turning the next page.

The freshly painted house, with its huge yard and many amenities, easily exceeded my expectations. It was in a charming neighborhood, too, and near a grade school. The new home caused me to reflect on the new state of our marriage as well.

Thank You, Lord, for allowing us to move here and for allowing us to begin anew, I silently prayed while unpacking.

Before I became a Christian, Ephesians 2:1-5 described my life perfectly:

> And you were dead in your trespasses and sins, in which you formerly walked according to the course of this world, according to the prince of the power of the air, of the spirit that is now working in the sons of disobedience. Among them we too all formerly lived in the lusts of our flesh, indulging the desires of the flesh and of the mind, and were by nature children of wrath, even as the rest. But God, being rich in mercy, because of His great love with which He loved us, even when we were dead in our transgressions, made us alive together with Christ (by grace you have been saved).

I especially appreciate the part about being "alive" with Christ. That's exactly how I felt after I took Harriet up on her invitation and accepted Christ. I felt alive. But I wondered what it meant not to walk "according to the course of this world." Eventually, I realized that I walk in the "world's course" whenever I try to control my circumstances. On that course, self—not God—is sovereign.

That was certainly true in our home. We desperately tried to control our circumstances so we could satisfy our selfish longings. These longings and expectations of life came from the heart which, according to the prophet Jeremiah, "is more deceitful than all else and is desperately sick; who can understand it?" (Jeremiah 17:9).

But praise God for heart transplants! As soon as I invited Jesus into my life, evidence of my new heart began to show. It wasn't as if I never sinned again, or that my circumstance-based viewpoint disappeared. But I felt God's Spirit—along with the light of His Word—guiding me like never before. It would be a l-o-n-g time before I understood that God is the only one who can orchestrate permanent change. But I definitely experienced a growing change of heart toward my family.

For instance, I realized that my children were gifts from God, not liabilities. How selfish I had been to view them as distractions from my goals. I was so deceived! And our children paid the price. Our son, Doug, had been exposed to years of arguing and strife. He was such a precious boy, but we were so preoccupied with our own lives, we didn't spend the kind of time with him he deserved.

I was determined to spend more time with Joani than I had with Doug. Even though I wasn't a Christian yet, I was older and more aware of the brevity of infancy. I smothered her in love and affection. But did I appreciate her as a gift from God? I don't think so. I didn't have that appreciation until I met the Savior.

Two months after I became a Christian, Orvey recommitted his life to Christ. From there, the Holy Spirit began opening my eyes to my husband's outstanding qualities—his kindness, compassion, humor, generosity, and unbelievable work ethic. I'd lie awake at night thanking God for this wonderful man, even though I was amazed that we were still married.

It amazed me more that I was falling in love with him all over again. For some reason I suddenly had an enthusiasm to meet his needs instead of only mine. That had to be divine. I couldn't believe it. I actually *wanted* to please him and looked for ways to encourage him and to make him feel appreciated. I even sat down one day and wrote him his first love letter:

Dear Orvey,

I just wanted to tell you how much I love and adore you. I appreciate all the long hours you work and the comfortable living you provide for us. I admire your work ethic, your love for me and the children, and your desire to become a better husband and father. Thank you for making it possible for us to enjoy so many wonderful family times together.

Love, Judy

I set the letter on the steering wheel of his car as a surprise. He called me from work in tears to thank me. He said he never knew I felt that way about him. It was only a little note, but Orvey has saved it for years because it started our healing process.

Another turning point happened shortly thereafter when Orvey's new boss invited us to church. Though the church was quite a drive from our house, we faithfully commuted every Sunday because we felt so welcomed and loved. For the first time in our married life, we attended church because we *wanted* to.

Soon our lives centered on this little church because it offered fellowship, involvement, and an entirely new social life. The only thing missing? Scriptural teaching. There were plenty of Bibles tucked in the pew racks, but they were seldom opened except for a "reading" from the minister. The sermons were entertaining, informative, and inspiring, but they had little to do with God's Word. However, with little prior church involvement, we never noticed what was missing.

During this time, I began reading the *Good News Bible* Harriet had given me. I found myself drawn to it with an insatiable hunger.

I couldn't put it down. It was like manna from heaven, and verse by verse it fed my hungry soul.

"Look, honey!" I'd say to Orvey. "Look what this passage says, listen to this verse."

Years later, I learned how important God's Word is to the believer. The apostle Paul explains why: "All Scripture is inspired by God and profitable for teaching, for reproof, for correction, for training in righteousness; that the man of God may be adequate, equipped for every good work" (2 Timothy 3:16-17).

However, at that point we continued to base our new faith more on feelings, circumstances, and expectations. No wonder we made a special effort to keep our past a secret from these fine Christian folks. We didn't want anyone to know we'd ever had problems. I told Orvey that we had found a new start in this church, so why would we want to share our tarnished past? For years we didn't. Instead, we put on our perfect Christian masks, partly to hide and partly to fit in.

And I went back to work because when it came to buying new furniture, a new car, or getting extra spending money for a vacation, I hadn't changed a bit. Even after we became Christians, landing "the good life" tempted us. After all, we had done without for so many years, I felt we had it coming. And we worked hard to keep it coming.

What came instead was a lay witness weekend conference at church. People arrived from all over New Mexico and Texas to share what God had done in their lives. We were encouraged to learn how many couples had survived far worse circumstances than ours.

At the close of the two-day seminar, one of the speakers encouraged everyone to go into the sanctuary and to pray together. As we entered that huge, beautifully appointed room, every light was turned out except a spotlight on the large cross over the altar. That light gave enough illumination for us to see that the entire place was empty.

After we made our way up the center aisle to the altar in front of the choir loft, we knelt at the railing and Orvey began to pray. "Dear Lord," he softly began. But he was interrupted by a man who had quickly wedged himself between us. The stranger put his arms around our shoulders and began to pray the most beautiful and powerful prayer I had ever heard. Scripture *flowed* from his lips. His words were like honey. What's more, he addressed specific incidents about our past and prayed about things we'd never shared with *anyone.* He knew all about the issues that had caused us so much misery.

Ultimately, he asked the Lord to heal our broken hearts and strengthen our marriage. And he challenged us to receive the fullness of God's forgiveness. His prayer assured us that Christ would never leave us or forsake us, and that His plan for our lives would unfold if we'd just seek Him.

Who is this guy? I wondered, *and how does he know all this?* I was tempted to turn around and look at him, but resisted because he was so loving and so passionate in his prayer. I didn't want him to stop. When he finally said Amen, we turned to thank him and— he wasn't there! We were completely alone in a silent sanctuary.

Through the years, Orvey and I have often shared the story of our mysterious "prayer partner" and what the experience meant to two young, impressionable believers. Was he an angel? Could it have been Jesus? I don't know. Whoever he was, God used him to point us to His Word, to His promises, and to His provision.

A few months after that special weekend, my husband and I celebrated our eighth anniversary with a romantic dinner. Afterward Orvey slipped a diamond ring on my finger. With tears streaming down his face, he thanked the Lord for our new beginning.

But it was *just* a beginning, for we were still stuck in a circumstantially based perspective. With no regular direction from the Word of God at church, we began to wander spiritually and vocationally.

Shortly after our anniversary celebration, Orvey got promoted again and placed in a rigorous management-training program that forced him to work nights. The long hours took a toll on Orvey's health. Because he wasn't getting much sleep, he was exhausted all the time and out of sorts much of the time.

I assured him that the training had to end soon, but it dragged on. What should have been a six-month stint turned into a nearly eighteen-month stint. Eventually, Orvey developed an ulcer and needed to be hospitalized.

Not surprisingly, he had slowly become disillusioned with the company. Because he performed so well in one phase of the management-training program, the supervisor didn't want to lose him to the next phase. Once again, we agonized over our circumstances. Should Orvey look for another job or continue trying to push forward in the current one?

The one bright spot in our life, though, was the purchase of our very first home! Working as a secretary in a large commercial real estate firm, I saved every extra dollar and put it toward the down payment. When I told the owner of the firm that Orvey and I were shopping for a home, he nonchalantly offered to write the contract and give me the commission.

I was overcome with gratitude. No one had given us a dime in our entire married life, so we considered this a stunning example of the Lord's gracious provision. Furthermore, our new white brick home seemed like a dream come true. It included three bedrooms, a living room, a family room, beautiful wallpaper and carpeting, along with a huge yard. Wow! We had arrived. *Now I'll be satisfied,* I thought.

We poured every ounce of our energy and money into that home. We planted a lawn, put in gardens, shrubs, flowers, and lots of rock to cut down on the water bill. It was great being a homeowner, but I thought the thrill would last longer than it did. *Maybe that comes when you buy a* bigger *home,* I told myself. Can you believe it? I still thought that more possessions meant more happiness.

Meanwhile, Orvey's night job continued to frustrate him. Finally, he decided to resign unless he got some relief from his grueling schedule. The company surprised him with an offer to take another position in Southern California as assistant manager at its largest facility.

"Southern California?!" I cried. "You've got to be kidding! Why would *anyone* want to live in Southern California? Isn't that where the riots took place and a major earthquake hit and where Charles Manson killed all those people?"

I had succeeded in squelching Orvey's excitement, but he flew to California anyway. He at least wanted to hear the offer. And while he was gone, the Spirit of God got hold of my selfish attitude and shook me by the lapels.

What am I doing to this poor man? I thought. *He's trying to improve our life, and I'm focusing on the bad press I've read about California!* I quickly made a phone call out to the office he was visiting.

"Why are you calling me out here, Judy? Is something wrong?" Orvey urgently asked.

"Honey, I want to ask for your forgiveness," I started. "I want you to know that if you want this job, and it means a move to California, I am right there with you one hundred percent. I want to be with you no matter where it is. We've asked God to get you out of these crazy working conditions, and He seems to be opening doors to do just that."

With my support, he took the job. And in no time, we were living in Placentia, California, in a beautiful four-bedroom home decorated in all my favorite colors. Having never lived around so much greenery, we were fascinated with the abundance of vegetation. Besides appreciating the lush yards and gorgeous flowers, we enjoyed our friendly neighbors and watched our children play together.

"Thank You, Lord, for providing such a wonderful place for us to live," we gratefully prayed. Because Orvey landed a management job with great potential, I was able to quit working—permanently. God *is* able to do exceedingly abundantly beyond all we ask (see Ephesians 3:20). We were living proof.

We had a great home, great neighborhood, great everything—except a great church. After we had tried several, a new friend invited us to a church in Fullerton. We jumped at the chance and discovered a parking lot as busy as Disneyland's. Cars were parked along the side streets for blocks. People arrived forty-five minutes before the evening service just to get a seat, never mind the *best* seat.

Besides the congestion, we also immediately noticed that everyone carried a Bible. We'd never brought a Bible to church in our lives. And we'd never talked before the service began, but these people were not only talking, they were laughing. After the pastor's sermon, we were hooked. It was so practical. Everything he taught was right out of the Bible.

I never knew there was stuff in the Bible that actually spoke to modern-day situations, I thought. *It seemed the pastor was speaking right to me!*

On our drive home my husband remarked, "There is something really *different* about that church, Judy. For one thing, you can hardly find a seat. For another, the people seem genuinely excited just to be there. I even noticed people taking notes of everything the pastor said. *Think* of that! Let's go again next week!" Go again we did, and by learning God's Word week after week our viewpoint began changing more and more.

CHAPTER 5

Forgiveness or Promissory Note?

⚓

*I*n California, we found sunny circumstances. Orvey had a good job, we owned a nice home, and we had just joined a vibrant, Bible-based church. But I have a *tremendous* capacity to store bitter memories. I store them in the *unforgiveness* section of my memory and haul them out whenever I feel like having a full-fledged pity party.

For years, I carried unforgiveness around with me like an extra twenty pounds. The heaviest memories came from when Orvey left to sort out his life. While he was gone, I felt incredible rejection and abandonment, even though he wrote me letters nearly every day.

Those letters contained lengthy explanations of why he thought we had had so many problems. There was a lot of blame, plenty of justifying, and a fair share of rationalizing. But the letters also contained many declarations of his love and incessant pleas for me to forgive him. He expressed vast amounts of regret over his leaving, and promised to make everything up to me if I would just let him come home and give our marriage a second chance. I read the letters over and over and, as you know, I finally consented.

What's more, within two years of our reconciliation, I became a Christian and my husband rededicated his life to Christ. God, through His amazing grace, gave us a fresh start. By then, I should have trashed the letters, those highly personal reminders of a miserable time. However, I secretly kept them in a large manila envelope taped to the bottom of a dresser drawer.

Whenever I was angry with Orvey and feeling particularly self-righteous, I read them and dwelled again on all the ways I had been hurt and all the opportunities I had missed. Orvey had asked me to forgive him long ago, but those letters dredged up all my unforgiveness.

Why didn't I get a dream-come-true wedding like so many of my friends? Why wasn't I allowed to pursue college, enjoy a carefree campus life, and realize my dreams? After all, wasn't I entitled to those things, too? I said to myself, seething with resentment as I turned the pages. *Why did I have to suffer for so many years at the hands of poverty and shame? Why did I have to sacrifice throughout my teenage years instead of having parents who provided for me? Why did I have to work such long hours at jobs I hated just to provide food for our family so my husband could play football? Why did my in-laws dislike me so much?*

Why did . . . Why didn't . . . Why wasn't . . . All the "whys" were eating my lunch. The result was bitterness—and one more "why." Why was I bitter? I was bitter because I did not yet realize that God had allowed that painful part of my life. He didn't cause it, but He definitely allowed it. And those unhappy circumstances were what eventually brought me to a place where I clearly saw my need for Jesus Christ and my need to put the past behind me.

In Philippians 3:13 Paul said, "I do not regard myself as having laid hold of it yet; but one thing I do: forgetting what lies behind and reaching forward to what lies ahead, I press on toward the goal for the prize of the upward call of God in Christ Jesus."

One day I would claim that verse to heal more. But for now, I continued harboring unforgiveness toward Orvey because I continued to read the letters whenever I felt frustrated over our circumstances. Never mind that God had blessed us with so much. Forget that He had provided so many friends, a fantastic church, outstanding Bible studies, a beautiful home, and the promise to bury all my sins as far as the east is from the west (see Psalm 103:12).

Someday I'll forgive my husband, I'd say to myself, *but today ain't the day!* To be honest, I loved feeling sorry for myself. Yes, I admit it. When I was "down," I could rationalize any behavior—including rereading those letters.

However, God put His finger on my unforgiving thought-life one winter day when I attended a Christian Women's Club luncheon in Fullerton. I listened in rapt attention as speaker Florence Littauer shared her life story with the roomful of women.

"I married a handsome, wealthy man," she began. "Our wedding was in *Life* magazine. After a short time of marriage, we decided to have children, and I gave birth to a beautiful baby boy. I named him after my husband. Within time, we learned he was suffering from mental retardation. He died before he was three. Our second son was born, and he had the same malady."

Her talk was woven with interesting details of her search for meaning and purpose in the midst of her grief. Eventually, the search led her to Christ, and He began to heal her pain. However, like all of us, she was also married to a less-than-perfect man and she struggled in that relationship. Only when she immersed herself in the Word of God was she able to understand the power of forgiveness and how that could improve her marriage.

Florence quoted 1 Corinthians 13, part of which states, "Love does not keep a record of wrongs" (TEV). Like me, she kept a list of wrongs against her husband—at least until she started meditating on this verse and forgiving him, one point at a time.

I sat in the audience with "ears to hear." After all, I'd kept Orvey's old letters—each one a long list—for years. But I'd never realized until then how damaging this habit had been to my spiritual growth and to my marriage. By keeping them, I'd kept my unforgiveness alive. The Enemy was doing his best to distract me from all that the Lord had done.

After Florence finished speaking, I drove home as quickly as possible, untaped the letters from the bottom of my drawer, and took them to our fireplace. I lit the gas logs and burned *every one.* My well-documented, carefully preserved lists went up in flames. At the same time, I prayed and asked the Lord to forgive me for the sin of withholding forgiveness from Orvey. I asked Him to give me His forgiveness for my husband. When I truly wanted that freedom, God set me free.

Do you struggle with forgiveness? Do you bury the hatchet, and then dig it up whenever it suits you? Do you enjoy feeling sorry for yourself? Have you been betrayed in your life? Abused by the people you cared about and who supposedly cared about you?

These days, I believe the most important questions I can ask God are not "why" questions. They are "what" questions. Instead of asking God, "Why are You allowing these circumstances?" I try to ask, "What do You want me to do in response to these circumstances?"

By keeping Orvey's letters, I let the unforgiven past shape who I was in the present: a deceived woman. Though I had abandoned the notion of divorcing Orvey when I became a Christian, that didn't mean I had abandoned the idea that I could pick and choose the circumstances I would forgive. However, that viewpoint leads to disaster.

Yet there seem to be more and more women abandoning their families to pursue a "prince." Most will tell you what a frog he became! When women trade their responsibility for a Cinderella moment, the affair results in damaged marriages and hurting children.

Still, when Cinderella moments turn sour, rationalizations run rampant. Some argue that they would never have had an affair if their husbands had loved them the way they should be loved. There's always the "I deserve better than this!" or the "All I want to be is *happy*" line.

I know it's easy to listen to what the world says is necessary for a happy life. Usually though, that has nothing to do with what the Word of God says. Still, how many times have I talked on the phone with a girlfriend, rationalizing my anger and hurt feelings by blaming them on something or someone else?

That response is easy. Seeking forgiveness, on the other hand, takes guts and faith. Why? Well, if I forgive the people who hurt me in the past, I have to take more responsibility for my present. Think of all the people you know who continue blaming their present troubles on their parents. "I can't help the way I am," some complain. "I was never properly nurtured."

I could latch onto that excuse, too. My dad was an alcoholic who didn't provide a secure family environment. At some point, however, I needed to come to terms with the fallenness of the world in order to forgive. I needed to accept that the world is out of perfect parents, perfect teachers, perfect husbands, perfect marriages, and so on.

Bookstore shelves are crammed with books that outline what it takes to be healthy, well-rounded people in spite of this fallenness. But what I really needed was in the Word of God. For Christians, the issue isn't about our needs. It's about Jesus. Is He sufficient for my painful past, my sins, my circumstances, my expectations, and my broken dreams, or isn't He? If He isn't, then He isn't God. His Word isn't true, and we have no hope. If we subtract God's viewpoint from our lives, we will become deceived, just like Adam and Eve (see Genesis 3:1-8).

Years ago I heard a noted pastor share a story of just such a deception. A young woman sought counseling from him because she had been sexually abused by one of her brothers—a traumatic experience, to be sure. As she related her story, she punctuated it with questions: "Why would he do such a thing to me? Why didn't he leave me alone? Why didn't my parents realize what was going on? How could such an awful thing take place? Why would *God* allow such a thing to happen to me?" Tears flowed as she tried to make sense of her troubled past.

After listening with compassion and understanding, the pastor spoke: "You can seek more counseling or you can have a breakdown or you can just give up on life and on God. But," he continued, "the final answer lies in the fact that you must forgive your brother in order to find healing and go on with your life."

"What?" she screamed. "You've got to be kidding! Forgive that miserable excuse for a human being? I want him to suffer in hell for what he's done." She ranted and raved until the poor pastor feared his secretary would think *he* was doing something to her. *"Never! I will never forgive him!"* she shouted and stormed out of his office, never to return.

Twenty-five years later, after this pastor had finished speaking to a large church in the Midwest, a woman made her way toward the front of the church. She introduced herself and refreshed his memory about their counseling session many years earlier.

"Tell me about your life," he gently inquired. "What has it been like since then?"

"Well, I have been divorced four times," she began. "And my life has been nothing but bitterness and pain."

"Did you ever forgive your brother?" he asked tentatively.

"No, I did not," she emphatically replied. "Actually, I can't. I can't give up my resentments and my bitterness. They're all I've got. I should have listened to you years ago."

Sadly, this woman chose to keep the fire of hate burning for all those years. If she had repented of her sin of unforgiveness, she would have no more excuses for her behavior. But she was angry with God and didn't want to change. When she turned away from Him, she turned toward her circumstances for help. With this perspective, she went from one husband to another trying to meet her needs.

I have often thought that I know better than God what I need in my life. But His ways are always best, and our ways are always second best. Worse yet, our unforgiving ways can lead to a lifetime of misery—something experienced by the woman who refused to forgive her brother.

God gives us the power to forgive all through His Holy Spirit.

But when we choose to disobey His commandment to forgive "seventy times seven," Jesus says He will turn us over to the tormentors (see Matthew 18:22).

Jesus goes on to say that the kingdom of heaven can be compared to a king who decides to bring his account up-to-date. In the process, one of his debtors owes him a huge amount and he can't pay it, so the king sells this man, his family, and all his possessions to settle the debt. But the man begs for mercy and the king feels compassion and forgives him the debt. This man turns around, after receiving this tremendous act of mercy, and goes after a man who owes *him* money, and refuses to forgive him. In fact, he has him arrested! When the king finds out, he is enraged.

> "And the king called before him the man he had forgiven and said, You evil-hearted wretch! Here I forgave you all that tremendous debt, just because you asked me to, shouldn't you have mercy on others, just as I had mercy on you? Then the angry king sent the man to the torture chamber until he paid every last penny due. So shall my heavenly Father do to you if you refuse to truly forgive your brothers." (Matthew 18:32-35, TLB)

Obviously, God thinks forgiveness is extremely important. When we refuse to forgive, we too find ourselves tormented.

That makes sense. When I refuse to forgive someone, I start plotting revenge—an activity that empties my heart of love and fills it with hate. The two are mutually exclusive. As John wrote, "If someone says, 'I love God,' and hates his brother, he is a liar; for the one who does not love his brother whom he has seen, cannot love God whom he has not seen" (1 John 4:20).

If, like me, you wallow in being a victim, it's time to forgive. To do so, you must believe that God is sovereign (see Psalm 103:19), that He has a plan for your life (see Romans 8:29), and that He wants you to trust that He is in control of that plan (see Philippians 1:6).

Romans 8:28 explains, "God causes all things to work together for good to those who love God, to those who are called according to His purpose." While I consider that verse one of the Bible's most hopeful, I also view it as the most mysterious. When I blow it and make wrong choices, when I haven't really sought God's will, when I have run ahead of Him with my choices, He says He'll work it together for good.

What marvelous, outrageous grace!

That verse tells me to stop worrying about my past, to stop asking "What if" and saying "Yeah, but . . . " God is committed to His promises. And He promises He will work all of our circumstances together for good.

What good could God possibly create in a life filled with painful circumstances? I don't know. God says *He* will work it out. We need to leave it at that. But in my case, forgiveness and healing from my discouraging circumstances made a platform for my ministry. For instance, when I gave God the broken places in my life, He used them to help me identify with others struggling with the same thing (see 2 Corinthians 1:3-4).

No one has the perfect life. Yet some give the false impression that they are good, wholesome people who don't sin. That's not transparent. And it's not honest. The Scriptures are clear: "If we say that we have not sinned, we make Him a liar, and His word is not in us" (1 John 1:10).

Being transparent means letting others see us as God sees us—as sinners in need of forgiveness. Admitting our sin and receiving God's forgiveness is the cornerstone of our faith. The Cross is where our sin was paid for and forgiveness was made possible, no matter how horrendous the past.

Most people want to take credit for their good lives. But the Bible says we have nothing for which to take credit (see Romans 4:1-5). After all, He is the one who planned how to redeem us. He paid the price. He sent His perfect Son to take on our sins and die a horrible death to provide forgiveness and restoration. By paying that kind of price, there is no wound so deep, so great, or so damaging that He cannot restore. No wonder it is called "the good news." It's *so* good it puts all other news on the back page.

If you wrestle with forgiveness, you already know it doesn't come naturally. Rather, it comes supernaturally through the grace of God. Furthermore, deciding to forgive isn't always like deciding to turn a corner. It can take time to forgive, even when you have placed a grudge in God's hands.

To this day, I struggle with being a scorekeeper. I still find myself pouting when my husband and I have a disagreement.

"Is anything wrong, Judy?" Orvey will ask.

"Oh, no. I'm fine, Orvey. Nothing's wrong," I will reply before giving him the silent treatment for another hour. The only time I don't talk is when I am sleeping, so Orvey knows my silence is a red flag. After all, it's very human to want to be right, to want to win, and to shy away from forgiving. In fact, our sin nature is bent on *withholding* forgiveness.

That's why Jesus, and the new nature He provides, is our only hope of consistently and genuinely forgiving. The eternal life He offers us begins with His forgiveness to you and to me. But sometimes it's hard to pass that forgiveness on to others, despite His explicit commandment in Matthew 6:14: "For if you forgive men when they sin against you, your heavenly Father will also forgive you. But if you do not forgive men their sins, your Father will not forgive your sins" (NIV).

The tall order comes because unforgiveness breaks fellowship with others and with God. In my case, it siphoned off so much joy and peace year after year. Unforgiveness cost me, big time. How much has unforgiveness cost you? Where could forgiveness happen in your life? As you contemplate, remember that forgiving differs greatly from *overlooking* wrongs:

"It's okay that you stole all our money in a bad business deal."

"It's okay that you were an alcoholic and mistreated our family."

"It's okay that you abused me."

"It's okay that you cheated on me."

Of course, it isn't okay. Forgiveness does not mean that you must excuse, tolerate, or dismiss pain. No. God knows the pain in your heart. If you deny it, you may fool those around you. You may even fool yourself. But you won't fool Him.

True forgiveness means honestly acknowledging the pain, then going one step further and forgiving the person who caused it—regardless of how justified you are in holding a grudge.

Forgiveness requires confession. A prayer of confession might be something like this:

> *Lord, I confess the pain I feel about the hurt done to me by _____. Please forgive me for holding onto unforgiveness because of _____. Please forgive me for trying to forgive in my own strength. Father, give me Your unconditional love for this person. Forgive them through me. Please give me peace, joy, and release from the bondage of this unforgiveness. I trust in Your Word and Your powerful presence in my life to accomplish this victory. In Jesus' name, Amen.*

Nothing comes closer to Christlikeness than forgiving others or ourselves.

CHAPTER 6

Hey, What About My Rights?

❧

I'm not exactly sure which day I crowned myself Queen of the Universe, but I think it was probably the day I was born. As long as I can remember, I put myself at the center of everything, and the world reinforced this selfishness. No wonder I made a royal fuss when things didn't always go my way in marriage.

However, today I wonder if I would respect my husband if he doted over me endlessly. How would I feel if he catered to my every whim, agreed with my every word, and offered no opinion of his own? Did I really want a husband who jumped when I said jump? Would I become disgusted with someone so spineless?

I wonder . . . would I appreciate the beauty in creation if beautiful things always surrounded me? Would I appreciate a two-week vacation as much if it weren't preceded by fifty weeks of work? Would I appreciate well-behaved children if they were never naughty? If I had everything I thought I deserved, what would my character be like?

Nonetheless, as a self-appointed Queen of the Universe, I felt I deserved both royal treatment and royal authority at all times. I asserted my royal rights most when my husband and I tackled home projects.

In one instance, Orvey and I decided to paint our house instead of contracting a professional. We couldn't wait to spend all the hundreds of dollars we were going to save this way. We were young, industrious, and energetic. Why hire someone when we could do it ourselves?

Because Orvey commuted to Los Angeles every day, I took charge of picking up the paint and a compressor—a machine that could supposedly save us oodles of time and energy. That sounded good to me. So I trudged to the paint store, picked out the paint, and reserved a compressor. The storeowner then introduced me to an older man who gave me a five-minute crash course on how to operate it. This employee seemed inebriated, and his directions didn't make any sense.

Yeah, yeah, yeah, I thought to myself. *You fill the paint bucket, pull the trigger, and presto, spray away. No big deal.*

That Saturday morning, I picked up the compressor while my husband prepped our house for this simple, one-day paint job. He power-washed the eaves, the wood siding, and the stucco. He covered all the windows with paper and plastic. And he was confident we'd be done by 6 p.m. to enjoy the fruit of our labors. Orvey filled the five-gallon bucket with paint and turned on the compressor.

"Well, here goes!" he announced. When he pulled the trigger on the compressor hose, the force nearly knocked him off his feet. Paint flew everywhere, blowing the plastic off the windows and spraying the shrubs and trees.

"Boy, this baby is powerful!" Orvey shouted. "I can't believe the pressure." He hunkered down, tightened his grip on the nozzle, and charged forth like a possessed warrior. White paint shot out, hitting the siding like a blizzard. In fact, white paint hit everything—our terrazzo front porch, the sidewalks, trees, shrubs, mailbox, and any unfortunate birds flying by.

"Honey!" I finally screamed. "You are *ruining* our home!" Orvey turned with a scowl on his face that could have scared Hitler. He pointed that nozzle at me, threatened to pull the trigger, and then sprayed me with a few choice words instead. I ran into the half-painted house crying.

By evening, our house was almost completely painted, as was half our neighborhood and three-quarters of my husband. His face was entirely white except for the area shielded by his glasses, which made him look like an albino Batman. Orvey stopped at 6 p.m. only because he ran out of paint, and the paint store had already closed. It was closed Sunday, too.

Nonetheless, we were determined to finish the job that weekend, so we sent our fingers walking through the Yellow Pages. The nearest open paint store was twenty-five miles away in Mission Viejo. Orvey insisted he couldn't both drive and clean up the mess, so I made the trek for two more gallons of paint.

"I cannot understand how we could have run out of paint," I lamented to the clerk. "We rented a compressor, thinking it would save us time, but the paint blasted out of the nozzle like water out of a fire hose and became hard to control." At that point, the man suggested reducing the compressor pressure.

"Wha. . . wha. . . what did you say?" I asked, feeling a bit light-headed.

"Why don't you just turn the pressure down on the compressor?" he repeated. "There is a knob underneath the back panel. If you have a compressor turned up too high, you'll use too much paint."

Suddenly, I recalled the inebriated man's instructions, and I vaguely remembered him mentioning something about a knob. On the way home, I debated over showing Orvey the knob. After I pulled into our driveway, I cautiously got out of the car.

"Honey, I have a confession to make," I said, "and an apology."

"What is it *now*, Judy? Can't you see I am busy?" he groused.

"Honey, I forgot to tell you about a knob on the compressor that controls the pressure," I blurted and then walked over and turned the knob from its current "blast-off" level to the more moderate number three pressure. "Try it now, *precious*," I gently and quietly said in my most righteous tone, hoping he wouldn't turn the nozzle on me. Sure enough, the paint flowed like a gentle Hawaiian breeze off the ocean.

That day makes me giggle now, but it wasn't very funny at the time. Our words and thoughts were anything but Christlike. The circumstances—which produced outbursts of anger, strife, and dissension—revealed what decidedly weak, sinful people we were. We certainly weren't communing with God in the garden that day!

Who's to blame for the way we acted? We could blame Adam or Eve or the serpent or even God. I could blame Orvey for not hiring an expert in the first place. Better yet, I could blame him for not picking up the compressor. After all, what kind of job is that for a *queen?* Should I have to take valuable time from my precious life to listen to instructions from some guy who's tipping a bottle of booze at 10 a.m.?

I am ashamed to admit that I've spent a good deal of my life defending my selfish behavior, demanding my way, and blaming others when circumstances go sour. So, what's new? Adam blamed Eve (see Genesis 3:8-12). Eve blamed the serpent (see Genesis 3:13). And they passed their sin natures onto the entire human race, including me (see Romans 5:12). It is the endless mystery of iniquity.

Mostly, I blamed my family. Early on, I adopted a victim mentality. Once I got into that mindset, I would hear the echo of the Smothers brothers' familiar words: "Mom loved you best." I was convinced my parents loved my brother more than me. That, I thought, explained why they seemed to shower him with more attention, more privileges, and more support. After all, he was the one who went to college. He was the one who traveled to Europe. He was the one who became a big officer in the Navy. He was the one who had the beautiful wedding. He was the one who had the opportunities to pursue a meaningful life!

For years I assumed my parents were *proud* of him and *ashamed* of me. I never felt I could capture their love or respect. So I grew more and more jealous of my brother, and he didn't even know it.

I could justify my self-pity and unforgiveness by believing what pop psychologists would say about me: I was a codependent adult child of alcoholic parents raised in a dysfunctional family. My inner child had apparently been adopted out. I was such damaged goods, I thought. No wonder I got pregnant. That mindset absolved me of all my sin, all my failure, and all my personal responsibility.

In this way, I dropped my sin off at everyone else's doorstep but my own. Then I learned of another place to drop it. I learned to excuse my self-centered behavior as the result of "low self-esteem." When that phrase got coined, I jumped on it like a frog jumps on a lily pad.

"Yep," I told myself, "the reason I haven't done more with my life is because of my lousy self-image." But as I began digging into the Word of God, I found no reference to low self-esteem—only references to how we adore ourselves, often more than we adore God.

For example, who's the first person you spot when someone hands you a family photo? I am immediately drawn to myself, saying things like "Oh, look how awful I look and how fat. Look at that stupid grin on my face. I can't believe how ridiculous my hair looks."

So what's the solution to this problem of rights, entitlements, and expectations? A shift from a human viewpoint of our rights to God's viewpoint. I needed to recognize that God allows circumstances for two reasons: to reveal areas in my life where I am not like Christ (see Romans 8:29-30) and to use me to bring His light into a dark world (see Matthew 5:14-16).

Choosing to surrender my rights has always been a struggle. After all, we live in an age that encourages me to assert them! We have women's rights, animal rights, children's rights, abortion rights, environmental rights, employee rights, disabled persons' rights, minority rights, and the list goes on.

That's the rub, isn't it? We want our way and we want God's will. But we are often unwilling to believe that those things may be mutually exclusive. One must die for the other to live.

Slowly, I discovered that Jesus wanted to free me from my self-centeredness, that He wanted me to step down from my throne and put Him there and abide in Him instead (see John 15:4-5). As usual, He led by example. For instance, He unselfishly left His special rights and privileges in heaven and humbled Himself to live on this earth. Once here, He did not exalt Himself as King. He could have exercised His power, but "although He existed in the form of God, did not regard equality with God a thing to be grasped, but emptied Himself, taking the form of a bond-servant, and being made in the likeness of men" (Philippians 2:6-7).

Paul encourages this Christlike attitude (see Philippians 2:5; 1 Peter 2:21) while John discourages us from having the attitude of the world (see 1 John 2:15-17). I read it and believed it, but took much more time to obey it.

CHAPTER 7

Growing Up or Growing Old?

❧

When I was a little girl, I had a disability called "cleanitis." I loved to keep the house clean, tidy, and under control—especially my bedroom. I kept it neat as a pin and decorated it with panache. The walls were piggy pink, and every six months I rotated matching bedspreads and curtains to keep the decor fresh. My bedroom represented something of my heart's longing.

Someday, I am going to have the house of my dreams, I thought. I cut pictures out of magazines and envisioned living in a quaint cottage in the forest with a white picket fence, green shutters, and climbing roses everywhere.

When Orvey and I bought our home in Placentia, California, it was big enough, but it needed plenty of personal touches. So I happily wallpapered the entire place and planted flowers. It was such a pleasure seeing the results of all my hard work, and I soon fell in love with our new home. Then my husband came home one day with the four little words every woman dreads: "Honey, we've been transferred."

I immediately pelted Orvey with questions. He explained that he had just been promoted to vice president, and the president needed him to work at the company headquarters in Denver—right away.

I was thrilled with his promotion, but my heart sank at the thought of leaving our home in California. In eight short years California had stolen my heart. I loved the mountains, the beaches, the desert, and the wonderful circle of friends we had cultivated at our church.

"How can we leave now?" I cried. "Doug is in his senior year of high school."

"He's either got to move with us or stay here and live with friends," Orvey replied. "The decision will be up to him." At first Doug agreed to move. But then he reneged and arranged to stay in California until he graduated.

With that settled, we began to pack. Even then, I knew I would miss our neighbors Randy and Kerry Fitzpatrick the most. We had only known them for a year. But we'd immediately struck up a friendship with this awesome twosome.

Randy traveled a lot for work, so Kerry was often left home alone to care for their two young daughters. As our friendship grew, I invited her to the Christian Women's Club. To my delight, she accepted Christ as her Savior within a short time of joining me at the meetings, and Randy made the same decision a month later. Consequently, the friendship between us grew into something extremely special and eternal. The guys would play golf while Kerry and I did what we do best. We talked. And the more we talked, the closer we became. It broke my heart to move away from these new, dear friends.

The move became easier when Orvey promised I could fly back to California in six months to visit Kerry and attend the dedication ceremony of our new church facility. It also helped when, two weeks after listing our home, we sold it for more than three times its original price. We'd never seen so much money in our lives. So when we got to Denver, we bought the biggest house our money could buy.

It was a brick beauty with three stories—four, including the finished basement. Inside, staircases, high-beamed ceilings, and a gorgeous family room with a large brick fireplace made it picture perfect. Outside we could gaze at the majesty of the Rockies from our redwood deck. What's more, compared to California homes, the yard was gigantic. It was also perfectly landscaped.

After buying this home, we had enough money left over for new appliances, new dining room furniture, and new office furniture. We also wallpapered every bedroom to our taste. Unfortunately, the thrill of living in an exquisite home soon wore off.

First of all, it's no fun owning a mansion unless you have friends to covet it. I had no friends in Colorado; they all lived in California. Second, I was homesick and couldn't wait to fly back to California as planned in six months. I remember the growing anticipation I felt as the plane slowly descended into Orange County, California. Once I had deplaned, I quickly spotted Kerry with her girls. Marcy, age three, broke away from her and ran toward me as fast as her short little legs would carry her.

I expected to sweep her off her feet and hug her with joy, but as she reached me, she continued running. In seconds, little Marcy had wrapped her arms around the legs of a woman at least a hundred years older than I. All the while, she gleefully screamed, "Judy! Judy! Judy!"

Had I aged that much in six months? Of course not. Physical aging takes place at a steady rate over time. Spiritual maturity, on the other hand, happens in a different way. It's not something we reach as the years pass. It can develop steadily. Or it can be stunted or slow. It can also happen in spurts.

While spiritual maturity depends on a number of things, regularly reading God's Word fosters growth (see 1 Peter 2:1-2). Yet until we meet Jesus face to face, we will never be fully mature. That process can be a long and discouraging one. But I am encouraged when I remember that when God begins a project, He is faithful to complete it (see Philippians 1:6). That's what makes the journey to Christlikeness so exciting. It's not only a direction, it's also a destination. Some people mature rapidly; others take longer. I happen to be in the slow group. That's why I must remind myself that direction is more important than speed!

As a young Christian, though, I wasn't aware of this process. In fact, I felt that once I had accepted Christ, I would finally live happily ever after. I'd heard of Christ's promise for the abundant life, but I translated that into "the good life." I actually believed God was The Almighty Aspirin that would take away all my pain. I believed He would give me the heaven-on-earth life I was seeking. But that wasn't God's intention. Rather, He wanted to work in me, mature me, and use me in the lives of others.

Eventually, I figured that God uses challenging circumstances to keep me humble and dependent. Psalm 119:71 states, "It was good for me to be afflicted so that I might learn your decrees" (NIV). In other words, affliction is the teacher, and we are the students. Charles Haddon Spurgeon once said it well: "I owe more to the fire and the hammer than to anything else in my Lord's workshop. When my school room is darkened, I see the most."

When do you see God the most? When do you pray the most? When do you spend the most time seeking wisdom and transformation from the Word of God? David turned to God's Word when he was hurting: "My soul weeps because of grief; strengthen me according to Thy word" (Psalm 119:28). Disappointments, afflictions, stress, and pressure all encourage dependence on the Lord.

When my schoolroom is dark, when my rose-colored glasses fog up, I naturally feel disappointed. However, these days I try to remember that God does some of His best teaching at those times.

Maybe your circumstances are starting to reveal your need for the Savior. Perhaps you've been living independently from God your entire life, and the trial you are now in has forced you to a place where you have lost control. Again, hopeless places are where God does His hottest work. Yes, it's a furnace, but just look at the gold that comes out of it (see 1 Peter 1:3-7).

In that furnace, God causes us to consider our life and our need for Him. Most people surrender their lives to Him during circumstances that are almost too hot to endure. When I look back on my own life, I can see how desperate situations brought about my surrender.

Besides leading us to Christ, trials help us grow in Christ. The apostle Paul says, "We also exult in our tribulations, knowing that tribulation brings about perseverance; and perseverance, proven character; and proven character, hope; and hope does not disappoint" (Romans 5:3-5).

Of course, God can change our circumstances in a heartbeat. More often than not, though, He allows challenging circumstances to bring us to greater faith. Trials make me feel "out of control." I, by the way, enjoy being in control. But when trials come, they force me to depend on God. You know what I am learning? That God loves me to depend on Him—for everything.

Here's another great passage regarding the value of trials:

Consider it all joy, my brethren, when you encounter various trials, knowing that the testing of your faith produces endurance [or patience]. And let endurance have its perfect result, that you may be perfect [or mature] and complete, lacking in nothing.
(James 1:2-4, parenthetical phrases mine)

Would you like your faith to be "lacking in nothing"? Would you like to be so dependent on Christ that trials can't defeat you? Those verses in James don't say *if* you encounter trials, they say *when*. Trials are inevitable.

Yet, it's amazing how the view changes when you look at a trial from a different perspective. In the late 1980s, Robin Williams starred as Professor Keating in a film called *The Dead Poets Society*. In one scene, Keating illustrates the power of changing perspective by asking his students to stand on their desks, one by one. That's what God wants to do in His classroom. And sometimes, He uses trials to get us off the chair.

What a different viewpoint Jesus had. The abundant life He

promised is not the same as the good life that the world promises. While one offers comfort, the other offers the cross. Jesus said, "If anyone wishes to come after Me, let him deny himself, and take up his cross, and follow Me" (Mark 8:34).

What is "cross-bearing"? Could it be the willingness to shoulder difficult circumstances? Or maybe it involves picking up new thoughts, words, and deeds—and dropping those less pleasing to God. In either case, not many Christians in America are interested in the cross-bearing assignment. In fact, the cross American Christians most frequently bear is gold plated and used as an accessory. But this verse in Mark is not about jewelry. It's about conforming to Christ's character, not our circumstances, in order to grow spiritually.

Romans 8:28 describes how this process works: "And we know that God causes all things to work together for good to those who love God, to those who are called according to His purpose." This verse tells me that even when I blow it, even when I get ahead of Him and make some bad decisions, even then He'll work it together for good.

Frankly, when the good times roll, I go shopping. But trials push me into His Word and onto my knees, more open to His will. Responding to tough circumstances this way doesn't make me feel happy. But I am learning that real contentment doesn't come from happiness anyway.

In the autobiographical movie, *Shadowlands,* C.S. Lewis expressed a similar sentiment:

> I am not sure that God particularly wants us to be happy. I think He wants us to be able to love. He wants us to grow up. We think our childish toys bring us all the happiness there is, that the whole world is our nursery. Something must drive us out of the nursery to the world of others, and that something is trials and suffering.[1]

Are you being driven out of the nursery today? Does it seem scary? If so, it's because the nursery is a comfort zone. And it seems absurd to leave comfort zones, doesn't it? But if we're serious about becoming like Christ, we *must* leave. God doesn't test us to see if we'll fall on our face. He tests us to move us from the nursery into the world of others.

As painful as the maturing process is, it is less painful than remaining immature. Immature Christians are easily defeated and easily deceived because they are spiritually malnourished.

It reminds me of the Rocky Mountain sheep living near Pikes Peak in Colorado. The tourists love to feed them popcorn, candy, sandwiches, and peanuts. But because the sheep were created to graze on grass, not junk food, they have become malnourished. The ewes can no longer produce milk for their young.

If Christians feed only on sermons about God, books about God, tapes about God, and music about God — instead of getting into the Word of God themselves — they will be spiritually malnourished and will remain immature.

Unfortunately, it has taken me a long time to mature in my faith. I have had great growth spurts, usually during trials, but then I'd get comfy again. Not for long, though, because God is faithful to His Word and to His work.

When we first come to Christ, we are baby Christians. New to that world, we find that our faith is based more on feelings, expectations, and circumstances. If life is good, we are good. But, like babies, we demand our way and fuss when we don't get it. Have you ever noticed how babies live to be served? Baby Christians are no different. Me, me, me!

Because we have little knowledge of God's Word, our faith is shallow. Paul describes the baby Christian in Ephesians 4:14: "As a result, we are no longer to be children, tossed here and there by waves, and carried about by every wind of doctrine, by the trickery of men, by craftiness in deceitful scheming." That's why cults feed on baby Christians. Baby Christians don't know the difference between the truth of the Word and the lies of the world.

Still, babies can be so cuddly and cute. Most people love babies. But no one loves an adult that acts like a baby. It's especially pathetic to see someone who has known Christ for years and has never really matured beyond the baby stage. Usually when baby Christians experience a trial, they holler, "Why me, Lord? Why this? Why now?" I did!

Paul speaks to the importance of growing past this early stage of faith in Colossians 1:28: "We proclaim Him, admonishing every man and teaching every man with all wisdom, that we may present every man complete in Christ."

In verses 9 and 10 of the same chapter, he writes:

For this reason also, since the day we heard of it, we have not ceased to pray for you and to ask that you may be filled with the knowledge of His will in all spiritual wisdom and understanding, so that you may walk in a manner worthy of the Lord, . . . bearing fruit in every good work and increasing in the knowledge of God.

The only way we can become filled with His knowledge and bear fruit is to be in His Word every day, letting it find a place to take root in our hearts.

As we mature in our faith, Christ makes a difference in the thoughts we think, the company we keep, and the decisions we make. That is the blossoming of the Spirit of God within us. In time, the fruit of the Spirit follows, evidenced by a life with love, joy, and peace hanging on the branches.

But branches need pruning in order to produce *quality* fruit (see John 15:2). As God begins the pruning process through various circumstances, the heart undergoes a transformation, which leads to a deeper commitment. At this point, true peace is realized. It happens when we internalize that God is sovereign, and that He works all things together for good for those who love Him and are called according to His purpose.

In my life, one of the most drastic times of pruning took place when our son, Doug, graduated from high school in California and moved to Colorado to live with us. He was as homesick as I was and deeply despondent. He didn't receive the college golf scholarship he'd hoped for, he had moved away from his girlfriend, and life wasn't turning out as *he* planned either.

Shortly after arriving, he began working at a restaurant and hanging out with less-than-desirable company. He started experimenting with drugs. The year he lived in Denver was a nightmare for all of us.

We made some calls and arranged for him to return to California where he could live rent-free in an apartment at our old church in exchange for working as the night watchman. He left in May with plans to enter college in the fall. We were grateful to see him leave his new circle of friends.

With Doug back in California, I felt stranded in Denver once again. I was still a baby Christian, and my feelings ruled. I complained bitterly to Orvey about everything. In the meantime, his company began to flounder. When the government deregulated the trucking business, the smaller companies were faced with steep competition from the megacompanies.

"Oh, God," I wailed, "why did You move us here? Why did You take us away from our friends, our church, and our support system? Why couldn't we have stayed in California? Now my husband may lose his job, and we'll never get back to our homeland. Oh, God, what on earth are we going to do?" Instead of placing my confidence in the Lord, I again placed it in our circumstances.

When you face a trial or uncertainty, what rules your life? Is it fear? Or is it faith? At that time, I felt fear and ran to just about anyone who would listen, hoping they would have the answer to our dilemma, which got progressively worse.

It was nearly two years before I began to run to God. It was cold and snowy, and the gray weather added to my gray mood. Still, I decided to go to a women's retreat at Glen Eyrie in Colorado

Springs. Glen Eyrie originally belonged to a railroad magnate who built a castle there for his bride, but she didn't like Colorado any more than I did and only visited the place once. Many years later, The Navigators purchased the property for its national headquarters.

My friend Susan and I were assigned the Tower Room of the castle. A circular staircase led up to a gorgeous room with a feather bed and vintage furnishings.

Our retreat speaker taught on 2 Chronicles 20. The fifteenth verse spoke to my heart: "Do not fear or be dismayed because of this great multitude, for the battle is not yours but God's." That's the verse the Lord used to renew my mind. It helped me realize that I had been battling my husband's job situation in my own strength instead of God's.

After spending some time on my knees, I surrendered yet another area of my life I was trying to control. When I stood, I had more peace about living in Colorado. I couldn't explain it. It passed all understanding. But I couldn't wait to tell Orvey.

Two weeks later, we were transferred to California. How shocking! Plus, our home sold in four hours, and we made another 50 percent profit—something we desperately needed in order to buy in the California housing market. Ultimately, we could barely buy a *dump*. We didn't care, though. God had brought us back to the Promised Land.

"Hooray!" I shouted with glee. "Now our troubles are over, and we can get onto the business of living happily ever after!" As I was shouting, God was sharpening His shears.

A few months after our move, Orvey faced a sobering dilemma. His company suffered a severe cash flow crisis and asked him to free up money by tampering with the retirement funds. He resisted on his Christian principles and decided the only option involved resigning.

"Maybe God won't notice, honey," I said hopefully. I figured God knew how much I needed the financial security Orvey's job provided.

Nothing doing. Orvey ignored my remark and resigned.

"Oh, *God,* my husband is out of a job," I sobbed. "Oh no, what are we going to do now?" All I could do was dredge up memories of my past. I dwelled on my dad's constant unemployment. Fear gripped me. Once again, circumstances were controlling my life, not God.

"God, don't You understand? I am a woman. Women *need* security. I desperately need it, God. I have to have it. Please, God, don't let Orvey be unemployed," I begged.

Within a month, Orvey landed a fantastic job and started driving the company car—a Cadillac. I'd always dreamed of such a car! But a year later, the company's owner suffered a massive heart attack and his son took over. Earlier, this young man had shown extreme jealousy over his dad's admiration for Orvey. Plus he was part of a large cult and began to systematically fire the leadership that didn't attend his church.

Orvey was out of a job again, and I was traumatized by dealing with his unemployment twice in one year. What was next? Was job-hopping going to be our lot in life? Was Orvey turning out to be just like my dad?

"Lord," I pleaded, "I can't live like this. I need security, stability, and medical benefits. Don't You hear me, Lord? Don't You hear me?"

Orvey got another job within a few weeks, only to lose it nine months later in a company buy-out. Once again, he was pounding the pavement, and I was livid. I bitterly related to Job's wife when she wondered what possible good could come of her husband's dreadful circumstances (see Job 2:7-9).

CHAPTER 8

Out of the Nursery

❧

*O*rvey lost his job during the first part of August, so we tightened our belts and tried to keep our expenses down. However, we had already purchased tickets to the 1984 Olympic Games, which were held in Los Angeles later that month. So we went.

Too bad I didn't enjoy this special event. I couldn't. I was too preoccupied with our circumstances and didn't understand that God had allowed them. Everywhere I looked, I saw gainfully employed people, and it reminded me that eventually we would be living on the streets with nothing more than the clothes on our back and our sleeping bags.

Have you ever looked at another Christian and thought, "They've got it made?" That person may have a great marriage, a wonderful vocation, children who love the Lord, and a rewarding ministry along with plenty of money and pleasure. What we don't see in those "blessed" people we envy so much is the trials they are presently experiencing. The trials are there all right, in some form or another. We just don't recognize them. God's purification process is different for each of us.

As the days dragged on, I felt more and more miserable and hopeless. I grieved over our situation. I wanted my husband to have a good job and for me to have disposable income. Like the persistent widow in Luke 18, I went to the court of heaven, demanding justice. "God, do You know what a wonderful man my husband is?"

I prayed. "He doesn't deserve all the unfair treatment he's gotten these past few years. How can this be happening to us, and especially to him?"

Meanwhile, Orvey seemed unruffled. "Judy, the neatest thing happened to me driving home from just being fired," he shared. "The Spirit of God spoke to my heart and exhorted me to trust Him and not my circumstances. I knew He was telling me to anticipate something extremely special in the coming months."

I couldn't believe that. Though by then I had grown substantially as a Christian, I still clung to financial security more than to faith. I held on to that area of my life like one would hold on to a life jacket on the sinking *Titanic*. Financial security was *everything*. Money was my god. Not because I worshiped it, but because I trusted it. I trusted it more than the sufficiency of God to provide for us.

But is God only trustworthy when the bank account is full? When the stock market is up? When the paycheck rolls in week after week? When the 401K matures? When the bonus comes the first of the year?

At the end of September, there were still no job offers. Not even a lead. That's when our friends Randy and Kerry Fitzpatrick phoned with an enticing invitation. "Why don't you two visit us?" they said. "It will do you good to get your mind off your situation for a few days. The tickets are in the mail!"

I didn't want to seem ungrateful, but they had just moved to Dallas, and Dallas in September is *scorching*—smokin' hot. Yet the trip turned out to be like a refreshing drink of cold water as those Christian friends showered us with their love, their laughter, and their encouragement.

"Trust the Lord, no matter what!" Randy said as he drove us to the airport. "He'll never let you down."

I figured I could do that. A job had to be just around the corner. But deep inside, I wondered *what* corner? I tried to muster up a positive attitude, but it had little effect. My insides still churned. Positive thinking is a more natural way of getting through tough times. I already knew a natural solution wasn't going to cut it. I needed something supernatural.

By the end of October, there was still no job. A lot more leads. A lot more résumés sent out. A lot more interviews. But no job. I continued panicking. Some early mornings I would wander downstairs and find Orvey prostrate on the floor, his face in his hands as he prayed. Other mornings I'd find him reading the Bible, tears streaming down his face. He was devouring some outstanding devotionals, books by men and women who'd been through trials of fire and had surrendered their entire agenda to God. I noticed Orvey's peace. It was as beautiful as it was inexplicable.

Then it dawned on me. A memory popped into my head, one that I had long since forgotten. It was a memory from a time when our family had gone to Mount Hermon Christian Family Camp. I had spent an afternoon by myself in prayer. I remembered asking the Lord, "Please make my husband the spiritual head of our home. He seems so busy climbing the corporate ladder; he doesn't have time to get into Your Word like I've been privileged to do." My mind came back to the present, and I gasped. "Oh no, God! Is this the answer to that prayer?"

Orvey was gaining peace from the living Word of God. As it transformed him, it strengthened him. And as it strengthened him, it comforted him. He was learning the truth not only about God's sovereignty, but also about God's faithfulness. How? Because he was renewing his mind daily in the Word. No longer were circumstances ruling his emotions. Now he was walking by faith.

And me? Well, you know me. My faith was based on my feelings still. And, believe me, they ruled like dictators. Furthermore, I didn't "feel" like surrendering those feelings to God. After all, I was angry. Didn't I have the right to feel that way?

When fear, doubt, and worry rule my life, I become more vulnerable to deception, and deception can lead to sin. I was at the deception stage, and I remember wishing I could just run away until

Orvey's stretch of unemployment ended. Then I would come home and start living again. Fortunately, our marriage was stable during that time, and I didn't run away. When the wolf was at our door, it may have affected us in other ways, but our relationship was as secure as a deadbolt.

"Two are better than one," King Solomon says, "because they have a good return for their labor. For if either of them falls, the one will lift up his companion. But woe to the one who falls when there is not another to lift him up" (Ecclesiastes 4:9-10). In our case the "him" in that verse needed to be changed to "her." Orvey was the strong one. I was the one who stumbled. The reason he was strong and I was stumbling was largely because of the difference in our viewpoints.

Orvey's perspective on our circumstances was much more divine than mine. He began understanding this season of unemployment as an appointment with God, who was accomplishing something in him that would have never been accomplished otherwise.

In November, Orvey still didn't have a job. Nonetheless, he put out a big empty jar with a pad of paper and a pencil next to it. For the next several weeks, our family jotted down the things for which we felt grateful—despite Orvey's lingering unemployment. Orvey planned on reading the notes after our Thanksgiving dinner to give God honor for all the other blessings we had received. I thought it was corny, but I went along with it.

By Thanksgiving the jar was full. One by one, we read the notes. Joani wrote, "Thank You, God, for allowing us to get to know Dad a little better." Doug wrote, "God, thank You for providing everything we need." Orvey wrote, "Thank You, Lord, for Your Word and for the comfort it brings during a storm." I think I wrote something profound like "Lord, thank You for Thanksgiving."

That day was difficult for me because the only thing I wanted to thank God for was a new job for Orvey. But that Thanksgiving there was no job.

December rolled around, and he still had no job. I went through the motions of putting up the Christmas decorations, but I wasn't in much of a festive mood. My feelings about Orvey's unemployment consumed me. The "what ifs" were robbing me of my joy. "It's no fun celebrating Christmas when you don't have a job," I moaned. "Besides, we don't have money to buy any presents."

Soon something wonderful happened, like what happened to the destitute Jimmy Stewart character in *It's a Wonderful Life*. Presents started piling up under our Christmas tree. Money showed up in the mail, anonymously. And remember my mom who had said, "You've made your bed, now sleep in it"? She and Dad sent us a check for two thousand dollars.

We received daily dinner invitations. Our friend Allayne Yackey gave us tickets to Disneyland. Grocery bags showed up on our porch, and we actually *liked* the food. Someone dropped off a load of firewood. We had so many honey-baked hams we could have opened a store. Other friends, the Mebergs, called daily with emotional support. Plus, commission checks from my sales job were huge that month. Usually, I only received one check a month from a lady who was poky about paying. That month I received three checks, and they more than covered our expenses.

We witnessed the truth of Philippians 4:19: "God shall supply all your needs according to His riches in glory in Christ Jesus." This caused me to wonder if we would have ever known the heights of His generosity if we had not known the depths of our poverty.

Shortly after that sweet Christmas reprieve, we awoke to the noise of our heater going on and off every few seconds. When Orvey checked the fuse box, it was smoking and melting. In a panic, he phoned our friend Kenny Witt, who worked for California Edison.

"Hey, Orvey. Don't worry about a thing," Kenny assured. "I'll send a crew out to fix it." Sure enough, the crew arrived and replaced the entire electrical box, upgraded it, and cheerfully left. We never got a bill.

In January, Orvey continued to job hunt. Meanwhile, I had to work at the semi-annual gift show at the Gift Mart. When a customer requested a bunch of catalogs, I left the showroom to retrieve them from a back-office bookcase. As I came around the corner, my arms fully loaded with the catalogs, I caught my foot on the edge of a piece of furniture and tripped. Unable to brace myself, I fell full force on the hardwood floor and hit the side of my face and then my elbow.

My tumble seemed to echo through the cavernous Mart. The bustling noise fell silent as all eyes turned to take in the gruesome sight of my body sprawled across the showroom floor. As I lay there in a state of shock, a wave of nausea swept over me. For a moment, I thought I was losing consciousness.

"Are you all right, Judy?" a coworker asked, running to my side.

"I think so, I think so," I answered feebly. I was so humiliated I wanted to disappear into the woodwork. Slowly I got up and felt my eye swelling. I looked in a mirror and gasped. My face was distorted, and my eye was almost shut.

I left the Mart immediately and managed to drive myself home, groaning and sobbing all the way. My arm was especially painful, and I found myself complaining again to God about my unfortunate circumstances.

I arrived home and was greeted by Orvey. Remember my athletic, football-playing husband? The one who majored in physical education in college? Well, being a physical education major to Orvey was like being a doctor. He took one look at all my bruises and my sore arm and quickly diagnosed them as bruises and soreness only. Then he gave me a prescription.

"Judy, I think I should turn on the Jacuzzi," he said. "If you sit in there with that hot water pulsating on your injury, it will loosen the muscles and allow the blood flow to begin healing your arm."

So I hauled myself up to our bedroom and began searching the drawers for my bathing suit. I took one look at my arm and wondered how I would get in, but I managed and trudged out to the Jacuzzi to be healed. I needed all of Orvey's support just to lower my aching body into the water.

After that ordeal, we quickly discovered that the Jacuzzi wouldn't heat over eighty degrees—a tepid temperature considering it was a forty-degree January night. Still, I sat there holding my sore arm next to the jet of water and shivering.

"Heal, heal," I commanded the water. But I was so cold and in so much pain, I couldn't stand it another minute. Getting out with one arm proved impossible, so Orvey lifted me from the churning water. I sobbed all the way up the stairs, took my wet suit off, and immediately went to bed, where I tossed and turned in pain all night.

The next day, Orvey detected the strong odor of gas coming from the pool area. After some investigation, he realized that we had a major leak. It wouldn't take a rocket scientist to deduce that we could have blown ourselves to the moon the night before. Saturday morning there was a knock at our door. When we opened it, our friend Clay Henderson filled the doorway.

"I hear you have a problem with the gas line to your pool," he began. "And I'd like to fix it for you." This was just another tangible way that God provided for our needs.

By the following Monday, I could no longer straighten my arm. So I made what is for me a major decision. I visited the doctor. "My husband thinks it's a bruised tendon," I volunteered. "My neighbor thinks it's a pulled muscle, and my coworkers think I've hyperextended my arm."

"Well, Judy, we have X-rays now," Dr. Hall said with a smile. While he was preparing my cast, all I could think of was *Oh Lord, why this? Why now? Lord, I am so tired. I am so sick and tired of all of this. Are you waiting for me to say "uncle"?*

Yet, two days later, another crisis hit. Joani called, hysterical.

"Daddy, I am so sorry," she began explaining to Orvey. "But I was mad at Skip, and I couldn't stop crying as I was driving home from school, so I didn't notice the red light! Daddy, I'm okay. But I'm not so sure about Mom's car."

The accident took place only two blocks away, so she inched my crooked, dented, banged-up car home. The insurance company declared it totaled. I was thankful she wasn't hurt, but I wanted to wring her neck!

"Well! Is this the thanks we get after all we've done for you?" I heard myself shouting after I realized she was not injured. Seems I'd heard that statement before, when I was a teenager and had made a wreck out of my life.

One discouraging thing after another happened during those months. We knew "the battle belongs to the Lord." But I was battle weary and could only huddle in my foxhole and wonder how much longer this war would be.

As I was sinking into this foxhole, my dear friend Luci Swindoll called. She knew of my battle fatigue and suggested that we harmonize to a hymn over the phone. She began singing "It Is Well with My Soul." Singing with her lifted my spirits. When we hung up, it was well with my soul. I considered this another tangible love note from the Lord.

After seven and a half months, there was still no job, and I had become a pathetic example of a Christian to my children. They knew I wasn't trusting God. I displayed little confidence in the same God who had transformed my life just fifteen years before. I am not proud of that. I just didn't know what God was doing or why He was doing it.

One afternoon, a friend left a copy of *Streams in the Desert* on my doorstep. Within the pages of this classic book, I found countless devotionals that showed how great men and women of the faith had responded to severe testing. They won their victory through surrender—surrender of their wills for His. George Mueller wrote the first selection I read. "What is the best way to have strong faith?" he asked. "Well, the only way to learn strong faith is to endure great trials. I have learned my faith by standing firm amid severe testing.

The time to trust is when all else fails."[1]

I turned to another page and found this thought initialed by H. W. S.:

> Nothing that is <u>not</u> God's will can come into the life of one who trusts and obeys God. Is it not a glorious thing to know that, no difference how unjust a thing may be from Satan, by the time it reaches us, it is God's will for our lives, and will work together for good?[2]

The common thread of each devotional was that God is sovereign, that He has a plan for our lives, and that plan is the *best* plan. Trials and adverse circumstances come into our lives so we'll turn to God, surrender our expectations, and grow in our faith as we watch Him work.

And what a sight it was to see Him work in my life — what a wonderful picture of faithfulness and persistent love, despite my unbelief. After all, for months I had wallowed in self-pity and viewed my circumstances from a "victim" mentality. I felt God had forgotten my family. As my rebellion increased, my faith decreased. The results were so devastating; I finally fell to my knees and wept uncontrollably.

"Dear heavenly Father," I cried. "Please forgive me for my rebelliousness and my lack of trust. Father, I surrender all. I give this trial over to You. Completely. Thank You for showing me that You are in control of everything. That You have a plan. That I can trust You no matter what is going on in our lives. Father, I am going to trust You from this day forward."

As those words fell from my lips, a sudden peace spread over me. It felt so wonderful. And so warm. Like a cup of hot cocoa on a cold, snowy day. Why had I been so stubborn? Who did I think I was, demanding my way when all along He wanted to give me something better?

As I prayed, 1 Peter 1:6-7 came to mind:

In this you greatly rejoice, even though now for a little while, if necessary, you have been distressed by various trials, that the proof of your faith, being more precious than gold which is perishable, even though tested by fire, may be found to result in praise and glory and honor at the revelation of Jesus Christ.

Our situation hadn't changed, but my viewpoint had. I knew God had a plan. My husband was still unemployed. But that day, I began to mature. It was a big step. I made a decision to trust the Lord—no matter what. For the first time in months, I felt joy. I had confidence not in our circumstances changing, but in an unchanging God.

After nearly eight months, Orvey still had no job.

We had peace.

We were down to our last hundred dollars.

We had peace.

What was happening? Something supernatural. God was at work in our lives, transforming our anxieties into His peace. He was also transforming something else.

On February 14, Valentine's Day, Orvey got a job with another trucking company! The tide had turned at last. What a day of rejoicing that was. It wasn't exactly what he had anticipated, but it paid the bills. And he continued remembering God's promise to one day give him a job he would love like no other.

After five months working for the trucking company, Tim Terrell called Orvey from Kansas City and invited him to interview at The Tom James Company, an international custom clothing company. We knew Tim and his wife, Dafney, before we moved to Denver, and then *they* moved to Denver and attended the same church.

"Do what?" Orvey replied. "Custom clothing? I've never done anything like that in my life."

"It's the greatest business on the earth," Tim assured him. "You'll love it more than anything you've ever done."

When Orvey hung up the phone, he was emotional. Tim's words had touched his heart. He couldn't imagine finding a job he could love—especially one in an industry entirely unfamiliar to him. Yet a month later he joined Tom James and attended sales school to learn everything about the custom clothing business. Orvey is a fast learner, and soon he showed an enthusiasm I hadn't seen in a long time. He couldn't wait to get through school and start working.

For the past fifteen years, that's something he's enjoyed doing as a custom clothier for The Tom James Company. Isn't God good? Turns out He was faithful, even when I was faithless during those long months of unemployment.

Remember how I disliked living in Denver? One day, it occurred to me that we found both our careers through connections from Denver. What a beautiful illustration of Romans 8:28: "And we know that God causes all things to work together for good to those who love God, to those who are called according to His purpose."

CHAPTER 9

Victory or Valium?

❧

*O*f course, I knew something of God's faithfulness before Orvey landed his dream job. It was just always hard to remember that faithfulness and rest in it. As a child, I tended to literally worry myself sick over circumstances out of my control—until three white pills changed my life.

Before I started taking them daily, it seems I was always fainting for one reason or another. I'd faint in the car, at picnics, when I was hungry, and when I was hot. My motto was "When in doubt, pass out."

I even fainted after singing a solo in the Christmas program. I was on the top row of the risers that evening, and when I toppled backward, it made a dreadful noise. The song was "O Holy Night," and believe me, that night the stars were brightly shining! Fortunately, only my pride was hurt.

My parents weren't the type to trot my brother and me off to the doctor's office much. But when I fainted in class one day, they scheduled an appointment immediately, and I underwent a battery of tests.

Little did I know that those tests were for diabetes, and the X-rays were to check for a brain tumor. I also had a brain wave test called an EEG to see if there was an abnormal *whatever* in my brain. I think my parents knew all the tests would come back clean. Nonetheless, we ended up in the office of a neurosurgeon in Albuquerque. He reviewed the tests and told me I would need to take a little white pill three times a day for the rest of my life. He promised that the pills would keep me from fainting.

For the next six years, I popped those pills faithfully. True to the doctor's remarks, I didn't faint again. After high school and marriage, though, I completely forgot about the pills. Then during a conversation about my health, Mom "fessed up." The white pills were placebos.

"Your fainting," she explained, "was caused by your constant worrying."

I suppose I should have been angry. But, indeed, I worried about everything as a child, and that habit grew leaps and bounds when I became an adult. Worry was my constant companion. By the time Orvey and I had been married a few short years, I developed more than fainting episodes; I had anxiety attacks, and worried myself sick on a regular basis. After all, I rationalized, my life was filled with turmoil. Who wouldn't worry?

"I worry because I am very responsible," I told myself. Oswald Chambers looked at worry a little differently. "Fussing always ends in sin," he wrote in his devotional book, *My Utmost for His Highest.* "We imagine that a little anxiety and worry are an indication of how really wise we are; it is much more an indication of how really wicked we are."[1]

I thought, *Let me get this straight, Oswald. You're saying I worry not because I'm responsible, but because I'm reprehensible?* Regardless, I wanted a second opinion.

After consultations with one doctor after another about my problem, I returned to the specialist I'd seen as a child. By then, I'd developed such a pattern of worry and episodes of dizziness, I was afraid to drive. When I told my problems to this physician, he didn't order any tests or X-rays. He simply gave me a prescription for a tranquilizer.

Do you know someone like me, someone who worries about everything? Is that person you? I was never the Queen of Serene, that's for sure. But I rationalized my worry because of my circumstances. I thought if I could only control them, I wouldn't worry. The problem? I wasn't very successful at controlling my circumstances, but I was very good at worrying.

Today worry addicts abound, and anxiety has become a national epidemic in America. It seems like everyone's life is on the edge, ready to fall apart because of stress. Some sources estimate that the clear majority of physician visits today are stress related. Curious about your stress level? Now there's a stress index to measure it. The death of a spouse is 100 points; getting fired, 47 points; moving, 45 points; having a baby, 39 points; going on a vacation, 13 points; Christmas, 12 points; and when an adult child moves back home, 8,000 points. (Okay, I made up the last item.)

Supposedly, reaching 300 points in a short period of time sets the stage for a stress attack. So the study recommends avoiding stress by controlling stressful circumstances. But how could anyone consistently do that? We live in a fallen world. The longer I live, the more out of control our world seems.

How can we escape stressful situations? For instance, how can we prevent the death of a loved one? Or prevent a mate from walking out? Or keep a job when our company is downsizing? How can we prevent a devastating diagnosis from a doctor? Or keep a teen from rebelling? We can't. Often we do the one thing we can do—worry.

Many say American society has never been more stressful than it is today for the following reasons:

1. We live in a high-tech age and are exposed to more information than we can digest.
2. There is never enough money, or there is too much money.
3. Jobs are more stressful. We're overloaded or being eliminated.
4. Debt is higher than ever. We're a nation of charge-a-holics. Some of us have black belts in Master Charge.
5. Economic forecasts fluctuate like the weather.

6. Marriages today are much more stressful because of blended families, working parents, and the lack of family support systems nearby.
7. Singleness is stressful and lonely.
8. Empty-nest syndrome causes stress.
9. Boredom causes stress.
10. Growing old is stressful, yet everyone wants to live as long as they can.
11. Retirement is stressful as everyone wonders if there will be any Social Security left.
12. Finding affordable health care remains a concern.
13. International terrorism continues to erupt around the world.
14. Environmental issues cause stress, too.

However, when it all boils down, worry is sin. Yes, sin—particularly the sin of unbelief. If I am believing the "lie"—I don't deserve this!—my response *will* be worry and anxiety. The result: unbelief. But the truth is, God is in control of everything in my life, including my up-to-the-minute circumstances. This understanding should change my response.

Please don't misunderstand me; I fully acknowledge that some problems are caused by chemical imbalances or glandular disorders. For these, you'd better see your family physcian. But it seems that the last possibility to be considered is always the spiritual—and only after every other possible natural explanation has been exhausted.

Our culture assumes that any problem related to the mind must be psychological or neurological. It's true that our problems *are* psychological. Our mind, will, and emotions, along with developmental issues, always contribute something to the problem and are a necessary part of the resolution. At the same time, our problems are never *not* spiritual. God is always present. Furthermore, it is never safe to take off the armor of God (see Ephesians 6:10-18). The possibility of being deceived, tempted, and accused by Satan is a continuous reality. Yet instead of considering our problems as "spiritual," we often turn to the wisdom of the world before the truth in God's Word:

- Psychic readers, the psychic network, or palm readers
- Horoscopes
- Gurus
- Relaxation music or aromatherapy
- Secular counseling
- Mind-control
- Visualization
- Hypnosis
- Self-help books and seminars

The media continues to feed us more answers to the problem of worry. But I feel the answer isn't in the papers. It's in God's Word. For instance, Jesus says,

> "Therefore I tell you, do not worry about your life, what you will eat or drink; or about your body, what you will wear. Is not life more important than food, and the body more important than clothes? Look at the birds of the air; they do not sow or reap or store away in barns, and yet your heavenly Father feeds them. Are you not much more valuable than they? Who of you by worrying can add a single hour to his life?" (Matthew 6:25-27, NIV)

Verse 33 reads, "But seek first His kingdom and His righteousness; and all these things shall be added to you."

Trouble is, I didn't think worry was a spiritual problem, so why seek first? I'd rather rationalize my behavior by making excuses. "Are you kidding?" we scream. "Do you have any idea how busy I am? Do you know what my work schedule is like? How about my kids' schedule, the demands my husband puts on me, my house, my friends, my workout schedule, and the committees I serve on?"

When we live with such schedules, we also live with the results:

lives consumed with worry. When I gave my life to Jesus Christ, He set me free from my past, forgave my sins, and provided a place for me in heaven.

"Thank You, Lord," I told Him, "but I can run my life, thanks just the same." Senseless, isn't it? But this was how I lived my life for many years after my conversion. I was deceived into thinking I could somehow control my circumstances and, as a result, control my emotions. But God never intended me to live well apart from Him (see John 15:15). And He never intended me to worry so much.

The apostle Paul wrote a lot about worry. Considering he lived with the threat of death his entire Christian life, this man was primed for a stress attack. He spent a lot of time in jails, too. But from those jails he wrote some of the most hopeful words that any of us could ever read:

> Be anxious for nothing, but in everything by prayer and supplication with thanksgiving let your requests be made known to God. And the peace of God, which surpasses all comprehension, shall guard your hearts and your minds in Christ Jesus. (Philippians 4:6-7)

These words tell you and me that worry and prayer are two opposing forces. If we are worrying, then we are not trusting. If we're not trusting, we are spending our time trying to handle things on our own. The result is usually worry. The solution to worry? Prayer. Prayer transfers the ultimate responsibility for my life over to God, who is capable of handling everything, according to Matthew 7:7-8: "Ask, and it shall be given to you; seek, and you shall find; knock, and it shall be opened to you. For everyone who asks receives, and he who seeks finds, and to him who knocks it shall be opened."

However, I was usually too busy to ask. And I wasn't seeking first—I was worrying first. Why? I had a ho-hum prayer life, that's why. At best, it was sporadic and tied to my emotions. So if I felt anxious, I didn't feel like praying.

If you had asked how long it had been since I shut the door on the distractions of life and poured out my heart before God, I would have been embarrassed. Worry—not God—continued ruling my life.

In fact, becoming a Christian made little difference in my emotional state. I failed to see worry as a spiritual problem. As a result, God couldn't give me the victory over my emotions that He mentions in Isaiah 41:10: "Do not fear, for I am with you; do not anxiously look about you, for I am your God. I will strengthen you, surely I will help you, surely I will uphold you with My righteous right hand."

If we're going to live anxiety-free lives, we need to begin by seeking God's strength through prayer and the power of His Spirit. Looking back, I can see now how God was working on this area of my life, using my circumstances to develop a powerful prayer life in me.

One of my most intense prayer times happened during the years our son, Doug, struggled with a drug problem. He lived in a cycle of abstinence and abuse. During one of his "clean" times, he fell in love with an adorable young lady named Cindy. He even led Cindy into a personal relationship with Jesus Christ. They had a spectacular wedding and all the ingredients for a successful marriage. Orvey was our son's best man, and I sang a duet with a friend. As with most marriages, though, problems crept in, and things began to unravel.

After they had a beautiful boy named Brandon, our son changed jobs. Nine months later, our daughter-in-law's mother suddenly died at the age of forty-five. A year later, Doug and Cindy experienced a profound financial reversal. Then, the following year, this couple had twins, Blake and Brittany. When the twins were seven weeks old, they contracted a catastrophic illness, spinal meningitis (and have since recovered).

Given these many stressful circumstances, I wonder how many points Doug and Cindy had on the stress index? After all, everything that could go wrong did. Soon the mounting problems affected their relationship and every area of their lives. That's when Doug returned to his drug habit.

Doug and his wife sought out a counselor, in fact many counselors. In time, accusations arose about our role as parents. We discovered all the areas in which we'd failed, and because of that failure, our son thought his problems were our fault.

These counseling sessions took place in the days when all the "experts" gave formulas for raising perfect children: A plus B equals PC (Perfect Children). We were told we got the formula wrong. More heated discussions with our son ensued, harsh words were spoken, and our relationship with him was severed.

Sadly, we were not only separated from our son, but also from our three precious grandchildren. The pain of not seeing them was agonizing. We could imagine them saying, "Where are Grandma and Grandpa? Where have they gone?"

Orvey and I were hurt, angry, and defensive. We knew we had made our share of mistakes, but how could we rewrite the past? Was there no hope because we had not been the *ideal* parents? Was our son's life destined for failure because, according to the experts, his needs hadn't been met?

Anxiety consumed us, especially me. I couldn't sleep. I'd stumble around our darkened house at night, crying uncontrollably. I lived in the past. I rehashed every conversation I could think of that we'd had with our son. During the day, I called my closest friends complaining, rationalizing, and crying.

Overwhelmed with guilt, I would cry out to God over my failures. The pain of those failures was a suffering I'd never known. Interestingly enough, when I shared this with our daughter, Joani, she'd respond with "Well, Mom, what about me? I don't feel that way about you and Daddy. Where was I when all this awful parenting was going on?" I wanted to take comfort from her words, but they didn't seem to help my broken heart.

Since then, I have come to believe that God lets our hearts break for our children who walk in rebellion so that we might better understand what it's like for Him when His children rebel. One day my dear friend Judy Svede, who'd earned the right to confront me, said, "Judy, what kind of a prayer life do you have? Are you spending time with the Lord? Are you seeking His peace and provision from His Word?"

"Prayer life?" I sheepishly answered. "I am too filled with anxiety to pray. Read the Bible? You've got to be kidding. I can't concentrate enough to read. It's all I can do to put one foot in front of the other."

Truth was, I really didn't feel like praying. Once again, I was justifying my behavior by my feelings. At best, my prayer life was inconsistent—even when I felt good. I bought those darling prayer notebooks at the store to add structure to my prayer life, but then I'd get distracted.

When I did pray, it was on the run.

About that time, a friend lent me some powerful tapes on the benefits of maintaining a solid prayer life. The tapes pointed me to the timeless Scriptures about the necessity of prayer. I was convicted of the sin of rebellion and independent living. Thus convicted, I decided to change.

I took my first step toward this change by confessing my empty prayer life for what it was—sin. Then I asked Him for forgiveness and made a commitment to get serious about praying. I searched the Scriptures for more verses on prayer, and one of the first ones I memorized was Philippians 4:6-7: "Be anxious for nothing . . ."

I love what J. Vernon McGee said about this verse: "'Nothing' is a very interesting word. If you have something, it's not nothing . . . that is not correct grammar, but it is an accurate statement. Nothing is nothing, and you are to worry about nothing." [2] Does this mean that we should look at life through rose-colored glasses, that we should avoid facing reality? Are we to ignore sin, sickness, and all other problems?

No. The apostle Paul says that we are to worry about nothing because we are to pray about everything. Of course, reading that makes me feel guilty. Sometimes I have done nothing *but* worry!

Yet, miraculously, the worry started receding when I started spending daily time in God's Word, renewing my mind (see Romans 12:2). I bought an organizational notebook and some classic prayer devotionals and got down to the business of prayer. I talked less on the phone and more to God. As a result, I slowly stopped looking at circumstances and feeling sorry for myself.

At that time, I prayed mainly for my son. God had me right where He wanted me and right where I needed to be. God became my refuge, my hope, and my help in this time of trouble (see Psalm 46:1).

Oswald Chambers once said, "Pray about everything. This solves the mystery of what to pray for."[3] By now, Oswald and I were becoming buds. And, indeed, I began praying not just about my son, but about everything. This helped strengthen my dependence on the Lord and weaned me more from depending on my circumstances, my emotions, and my longings.

Still, some days I would finish praying and take back all the burdens I had just unloaded. As soon as I began losing my peace, though, I knew it was time to seek the Lord. And I knew that "He is a rewarder of those who seek Him" (Hebrews 11:6). So I prayed with open hands, fully expecting God to make good on that promise.

The apostle Paul was my mentor in how to seek God. In Philippians 4:6, he says, "In everything by prayer and supplication with thanksgiving let your requests be made known to God." The phrase "supplication with thanksgiving" simply means we are thanking God today for what He is going to do tomorrow. In one of those tomorrows, He's going to answer prayer. We may disagree with His answer, but He does answer them. All of them (see John 14:13-14).

Each morning before I opened a newspaper, made a phone call, or had a good cry, I read Psalms. I made notes about the ones that spoke to my heart, and I claimed God's promises. I was amazed at the soothing effect His Word had. I never realized how much He loved me. Then I confessed my sins so I could begin my prayer time with a clean heart. I stopped trying to defend myself, and I surrendered control to Him.

But that surrender continued to be a hard-fought battle. For months, I had essentially been telling God that I didn't think He could handle my situation. If He could, I wanted dates. When, exactly, was He going to deal with it?

Eventually, I realized that God has a lot of spoiled children. I was certainly one of them. I would pout and say, "I have these unanswered prayers, God, so get with it . . . and be sure to do it on my terms."

When I heard myself praying like that, I became convicted and convinced that it was more important *how* I prayed than *how much* I prayed. So I changed the tone of my prayers. Instead of praying with a complaining spirit, I prayed with a grateful spirit. As I prayed that way, I noticed a transformation taking place. I began to feel a measure of peace in the midst of painful circumstances. A *measure* of peace? Why not total peace? Well, I still hadn't unconditionally surrendered to God. Before, I hadn't considered worry as a spiritual battle. I learned, maybe for the first time, that my battle was not with flesh and blood but with the Enemy himself (see Ephesians 6). I discovered that anxiety and fear are not from God. No wonder I was experiencing defeat.

When I realized it was a battle, I realized something else. It was a battle that needed to be fought from a strategic place—on my knees. After only a few weeks of consistent, fervent prayer, I began picturing myself walking up to an altar, much like Abraham, and placing my dear son there. I placed Doug's wife and their three babies alongside him.

Then I whispered, "Lord, I surrender them into Your capable hands. You can meet all of my needs and theirs, according to Your riches in Christ Jesus. I believe that. I also believe that You know all the desires of my heart. If You thought I had to have this family now in order to survive, I know You would give them to me. So I choose to leave all of that in Your hands."

What happened next was what I'd been searching for. Peace. It was a gift from the Holy Spirit. I felt such peace I could have been the poster child for Psalm 34:4: "I sought the Lord, and He answered me, and delivered me from all my fears." How did He deliver me? Through prayer. As James 5:16 says, "The prayer of a righteous man is powerful and effective" (NIV).

Powerful and effective prayer. How can we ever experience that kind of power unless we first experience utter dependence on our God? He is our Shepherd; we are His sheep. He is the Potter; we are the clay. He is our Master; we are His servants. He is all we need. But, as Ron Mehl wrote in *Surprise Endings,* "He never truly becomes all we need until we realize He's all we have." [4]

Orvey and I were slowly learning what Paul so eloquently expresses in 2 Corinthians 1:8-10:

> We were under great pressure, far beyond our ability to endure, so that we despaired even of life. Indeed, in our hearts we felt the sentence of death. But this happened that we might not rely on ourselves but on God, who raises the dead. He has delivered us from such a deadly peril, and he will deliver us. (NIV)

God was all I had. I believed that. It fed the roots of my faith, and I grew as never before. Each day I was filled with this unbelievable peace, even though our circumstances hadn't changed. Friends marveled at the change in my attitude. There were actually days during that yearlong separation when I didn't give our son and his family much thought aside from praying for them.

Then one day, one glorious day, our lost sheep came home to the Shepherd. He came home to his family. And he came home to his parents.

Jesus tells us about a homecoming similar to ours:

"What man among you, if he has a hundred sheep and has lost one of them, does not leave the ninety-nine in the open pasture, and go after the one which is lost, until he finds it? And when he has found it, he lays it on his shoulders, rejoicing. And when he comes home, he calls together his friends and his neighbors, saying to them, 'Rejoice with me, for I have found my sheep which was lost!' I tell you that in the same way, there will be more joy in heaven over one sinner who repents, than over ninety-nine righteous persons who need no repentance." (Luke 15:4-7)

Our heavenly Father is such a wonderful Shepherd, isn't He? He goes after the one who is lost. Until He gets tired? Until it gets dark? Until He gets discouraged? No. Until He finds it. And when He finds it, He restores it to the flock.

The Father sent His Son to die on the cross so that He could find us and restore us to His flock. He's at work every day restoring lost souls, damaged families, broken relationships, and broken hearts.

The restoration with our son was beyond our dreams. We called our friends who'd spent years praying for him. Then we killed the fatted calf, put the royal robe on him, gave him the gold ring, and celebrated his safe return (see Luke 15:22-23).

Today our son is a living testimony of God's miraculous transforming power. He is an answer to prayer. He walks with the Lord, as does his wife. We have witnessed miracles in our relationship with them. God is using both of them in wonderful ways to give hope and encouragement to other struggling couples. He truly has returned what the locust had eaten (see Joel 2:25).

I realized that during much of this trial with my son, I too had been living like a prodigal. I had wandered away from the only source that could help me. But prayer changes things. That's why God asks us to pray and not faint, to persist and not quit, to trust in Him and wait upon Him until He brings it to pass—whatever "it" is.

CHAPTER 10

Contentment in a Crowded Heart

❧

*P*at and I immediately noticed the late-model luxury car that pulled in front of her gift store. Then two young men — handsome and extremely well dressed — got out and approached the door.

When Pat told the gentlemen that the store wasn't open yet, they insisted that they needed to buy something immediately. Pat cautiously unlocked the door as she listened to their plea. "We need to buy a wooden watermelon slice right away," one of the men said. He then held up a carved example of what he was looking for. He was wearing a very expensive diamond watch and a huge diamond ring.

"I had items like that at the beginning of the summer season," Pat explained, "but I don't think I have any left. Please give me a minute to check the sale table." Pat scoured a table piled with marked-down merchandise, but she couldn't find one.

Out of the blue, the man began to cry. "You don't understand. I simply *must* find a watermelon slice like this one," he pleaded. "When my fiancée was in the hospital, I gave her this watermelon slice. She set it on her bedside table, saying it reminded her of my love for her. She just passed away, and her funeral is in two hours. I want to put another watermelon slice in her coffin so I can keep this one for myself, as a reminder." By now, he was sobbing. Pat looked at me, not knowing what to say.

"I have a whole collection of folk-art watermelons at home," I tentatively began. "And I only live a few miles away. I would be happy to drive home and get one for you."

At the offer, the man threw his arms around me in a grateful hug. "Thank you so much," he said. "You'll never know what this means to me."

I made my way quickly to my car and started for home. I'd been a sales rep in the gift industry for many years, and that day I just happened to be calling on my favorite store in Yorba Linda when we were interrupted by this man's visit. During the drive home I began wondering if our meeting was a "divine appointment."

I continued contemplating this man's pain and his seemingly hopeless situation. Was he trying to make sense out of her death? Could a silly watermelon slice bring him a measure of comfort? Or was this an opportunity for me to impart the truth of God's love to someone consumed with grief? I couldn't help but feel gratitude that, for the Christian, death is not a hopeless end but an endless hope.

Suddenly, I remembered the booklet I'd discovered just a few days before while cleaning out a closet. My pastor, Charles Swindoll, wrote *Destiny* as a power-packed explanation of the gospel of Jesus Christ and an assurance that if we know Him, we can spend eternity with Him in heaven.

That's it, I thought, *I'll give this man that booklet.* I pulled into my driveway, dashed into the house, grabbed the wooden watermelon slice, retrieved the booklet, and sped back to Pat's store. When I arrived, the man was slumped in a chair close to the front door. His head was resting in his hands, and he was quietly crying. I noticed his companion was near the back of the store whispering to Pat. I walked over and gingerly put my hand on the grieving man's shoulder.

"Here's the watermelon slice I promised you," I started. "I know this is an especially difficult time in your life. I have a little booklet I'd like to give you that has been written by a friend. I hope that in the days to come you'll read it. I believe it will give you great hope for your future."

The man stood slowly, took the items, and thanked me again before motioning to his friend and driving away. Pat and I stood in silence for several seconds. We were both contemplating what had just taken place. Finally, Pat spoke.

"Judy, you don't know the rest of the story. It seems this man's fiancée had terminal cancer. When faced with the prospect of grueling treatments with no real assurance of a cure, she took her life by hanging herself in her boyfriend's garage. He found her when he was opening the garage door." I gasped in disbelief and stunned silence as I pictured the gruesome event.

"Pat, what a wonderful opportunity we had today to share Christ's love with someone hurting so much," I finally said. "Jesus tells us to merely sow the seed. *Today* it was watermelon seeds." We hugged each other and cried.

I never saw the man again, but I've often remembered him. According to the world's standards, he seemed to have had it all—material success, good looks, and the love of a woman. He had everything. But everything wasn't enough. All his everything didn't have the power to prevent this tragedy, and it didn't have the power to get him through it.

Others have nothing, or very little, when compared to this man's circumstances. Yet they have genuine lasting contentment because of their faith. For instance, I know a content man who lives in a small community in southern New Mexico where the weather is hot and arid much of the year. In the winter, it's windy and frigid.

This community exists by a huge man-made lake. Some of the homes are modest. Some are big with well-kept yards. Others are run down. Most of the bigger ones belong to people who use them only for vacations. The rest of the population consists of lower-income residents.

The man I know lives in a modest mobile home on a gravel lot.

He has some rose bushes and a few trees, and he can see the lake in the distance. He lives on Social Security and on money from odd jobs. He doesn't draw a pension, doesn't have a 401K, and doesn't collect dividends from stocks.

He drives an old truck, has an old dog to keep him company, and spends hours making treasures out of wood in a little shed by the mobile home. He gets in a golf game whenever he can, but he's too busy to play as much as he would like.

When he and his wife retired, they moved down by the lake with the help of their daughter and son-in-law. The promise of a new beginning appealed to them. Sadly, his wife was ill most of that time, and he was left to carry a lot of the load alone. Seems a good portion of their married life had been filled with hardship and struggle, but in spite of that, they remained faithful to each other.

A few weeks into their "retirement," he was asked to step into the pulpit of a small, struggling church in the nearby town. He had pastored several small churches and was ready for a little break, but he felt the Lord calling him once again. He finally agreed, and soon he took on all of the responsibilities.

Besides pastoring the flock, he cleaned the church. He was the one who showed up two hours before the service to turn on the furnace or the air-conditioner. He visited the sick and counseled the brokenhearted. He shopped for the potlucks, headed up the vacation Bible school teaching team, and made crafts for the kids. He would rejoice when one person came forward to accept Christ. He grieved when issues threatened to split the church. Still, he kept doing his part. And God kept doing His.

One spring, he and his wife celebrated their fifty-fifth wedding anniversary. She was ill and mostly bedridden, but he managed to take her on a short drive and out for a nice dinner. About a month and a half after their anniversary, she died. It seemed so sudden and unexpected, but he knew God had it all in His hands.

Although deeply sorrowful, he preached at her funeral, as did his son and grandson. They wept, but not as those who have no hope. He knew she was in the arms of Jesus and that she was well for the first time in years.

He went back to his little home to grieve. But he kept on preaching every Sunday, kept on visiting the sick, and kept up the house and the laundry. He played with his dog, watered the roses, and worked in his wood shop. During holidays, he visited his son. Of course, he missed his wife terribly. They had been married since he was seventeen.

As time went on, he resigned from full-time ministry. But he continued filling in at other small churches as needed. Today he teaches a Bible study and attends local civic meetings and church potlucks. He still builds things in his shop, but he's also learning how to use a computer. He continues to work as a handyman. He spends lots of time in prayer, and even more time studying God's Word.

One day I asked him how I could pray for him.

"Oh, honey, I tell ya, the Lord is so faithful," he answered. "He's been so good to me. There isn't a thing I need. I have Him, and He's never left me wanting for more. In fact, He's given me more than I have ever asked or dreamed."

Now that's contentment!

How do I know this man? He's my father-in-law. He's seventy-five, and he has more energy and enthusiasm for life than most people half his age. As far as God's purpose for him is concerned, he'll never retire.

When he visits, he brings his tools and fixes all the things on my list. He's quick to bring us all handcrafted gifts, and he is appreciative of the home-cooked meals I fix him. He heads to bed around 9 p.m. with his sword—the Word of God—tucked under his arm. He never hits the pillow without spending a little more time with Jesus. He loves Him with all of his heart, all of his soul, and all of his mind.

I love this man. I admire his tenacity. He's had one hard life, and has made plenty of mistakes along the way. But he doesn't agonize over the past. He keeps his eyes on the goal. And he's content. But not from what the world has had to offer. No sir, he's got the kind that money can't buy and the world can't provide. Let's face it. Just living seventy-five years with the name Orvey Euclid Hampton, Sr., would be enough of a challenge for most of us.

He's learned the secret to contentment. He's learned that contentment has nothing to do with circumstances and everything to do with Jesus.

Most of the world can more easily relate to King Solomon's pursuit to have it all. We still believe we can attain that goal, and in this way find contentment. Ecclesiastes tells that Solomon pursued the good life, and that there wasn't much he didn't experience in the pursuit—wine, riches, property, vineyards, women, power. He was a man who had it all. Or almost had it all, for he pursued it all without God. And without God he found all his pursuits were like chasing the wind. He could never quite catch it and only ended up empty-handed. It didn't satisfy. Without God, nothing does.

Jesus said, "What does it profit a man to gain the whole world, and forfeit his soul?" (Mark 8:36). Paul taught in Philippians 4 that we can *learn* to be content no matter what our circumstances are. That's only possible, though, with a heart that is surrendered to Christ. That's what makes biblical contentment so unique. It's available only to the believer. Which begs the question: "Why are so many believers discontented?"

Some lose contentment when they become driven to nab the next accomplishment. That doesn't mean contentment excludes ambition. God doesn't want us to sit around as lazy, complacent, apathetic people trying to muster up contentment. Rather, Paul says, we are to run the race, reaching toward the goal. But contentment will drain away if these efforts are motivated by selfishness.

One of the best ways to learn contentment is to let go of the entanglements mentioned in Hebrews 13:5: "Let your character be free from the love of money, being content with what you have; for He Himself has said, 'I WILL NEVER DESERT YOU, NOR WILL I EVER FORSAKE YOU.'" The apostle Paul provides some equally challenging words in 1 Timothy 6:8: "If we have food and covering, with these we shall be content."

Ever noticed how opposite those truths are from what the world says? Ads all hint at a higher level of contentment than what we currently have. For instance, if you can eat the finest food, wear the latest fashions, drive the newest luxury car, live in the most wonderful area of the city, travel to far-off places, be physically fit, and decorate your home in style, *then* you will be happy.

I must admit there was a time when I desired all those things and believed I could find contentment through them. Through hard work, Orvey and I even acquired some of that package. All that did, though, was pressure me to acquire more. And that pressure didn't feel like contentment.

"More," I discovered, is not the secret of contentment. Paul says, "I have learned the secret of being filled and going hungry, both of having abundance and suffering need" (Philippians 4:12). He knew what it was like to eat with kings and to ride in chariots. He also knew what it was like to sleep under a bridge. He knew what it was like to freely travel among the churches. He also knew what it was like to be imprisoned in chains. He knew what it was like to be respected. He also knew what it was like to be ridiculed.

Paul truly knew the secret of contentment. It wasn't the absence of adverse circumstances, and it wasn't the ability to control circumstances. It was an inside job. He found it in Christ, not in trying to satisfy the insatiable appetites of the flesh. In Galatians 5:16 he notes the incompatibility: "Walk by the Spirit, and you will not carry out the desire of the flesh."

What deeds and desires does the flesh produce? In that same chapter, Paul lists them: "immorality, impurity, sensuality, idolatry, sorcery, enmities, strife, jealousy, outbursts of anger, disputes, dissensions, factions, envyings, drunkenness, carousings, and things like these" (verses 19-21).

Maybe you are thinking, *Mercy, I'm glad I don't struggle with many of those issues.*

Oh really? What about envy? Ever wished you lived in Southern California with a view of the ocean? Or maybe in a mountaintop chalet in Colorado? What about a second home? Maybe one in Maui? Or a penthouse in New York City, just in case you want to catch a Broadway play some weekend and have dinner at a posh restaurant?

What about jealousy? Ever struggled with that? How about wishing for the good looks and perfect figure of a movie star? A little less here, a little more there? Come on. Be honest!

How about immorality? Ever looked at someone else's mate and daydreamed about a fling? Wouldn't it be nice to have a little romance back in your life?

Ever thought about witchcraft? Ever read a horoscope? Ever wanted to figure out your life through a television psychic? Or played a board game that predicts your future?

The deeds of the flesh result in the death of contentment. Why? Because sin always leads to separation from God. Although it doesn't mean a loss of salvation for the believer, it does mean a loss of fellowship.

The solution is to turn from our sin and turn to the Savior. Ask Him for forgiveness, and you'll find Him faithful (see 1 John 1:9). If we don't, our hearts grow cold, and we wander away from the Lord.

"At the heart of the problem, is the problem of the heart," according to Warren Wiersbe in his book *Being a Child of God.*[1] The bad news is that the heart is desperately wicked. The good news is that the power of the Holy Spirit is available to help us find contentment—the kind money cannot buy, circumstances cannot produce, and pleasure cannot provide—deep within our hearts.

But like everything in life, we must do our part, and God must do His. Every day we need to renew our mind in the Word of God. Paul writes:

> Whatever is true, whatever is honorable, whatever is right, whatever is pure, whatever is lovely, whatever is of good repute, if there is any excellence and if anything worthy of praise, let your mind dwell on these things. The things you have learned and received and heard and seen in me, practice these things; and the God of peace shall be with you. (Philippians 4:8-9)

How many of us dwell on things that are truly "true"? Far more, I suspect, dwell on what the world offers as true. And these "truths" seem mighty appealing at times as they support selfish desires.

Developing a renewed mind is the best way to resist buying into this deception. Paul wisely writes:

> I urge you therefore, brethren, by the mercies of God, to present your bodies a living and holy sacrifice, acceptable to God, which is your spiritual service of worship. And do not be conformed to this world, but be transformed by the renewing of your mind, that you may prove what the will of God is, that which is good and acceptable and perfect. (Romans 12:1-2)

This "dying to self" that Paul talks about in Romans 12 is what brings contentment. That's the bottom line. That's how Christ infuses His life into ours. When that happens, it produces contentment.

But dying to self often presents a difficult daily battle, sometimes even a minute-by-minute battle. Usually when I lose that battle, it is because I have taken my eyes off Christ and focused them on my circumstances.

"You don't think God will really take care of all your needs, do you?" the Enemy whispers. "What about your job? Do you think it is going to last *forever?* And your children? Do you know how unsafe it is out there? Any good parent would be worried. Do you think you will be able to retire? What about your health? What about rising medical costs? And the economy? Good times won't last forever."

If I listen long enough, I find myself *under the circumstances,* and that is where I lose my contentment. But lasting contentment is not a state of affairs. It is a state of mind—a mind that is fixed not on circumstances, but on Christ.

If I believe circumstances are sovereign, I'll get stressed out. If I believe God is sovereign, I'll gain strength. And the more time I spend in His Word, the more I learn of His sovereignty.

If Paul focused on his circumstances and how terrible they were, I doubt he could have ever written the book of Philippians. He wrote that hopeful book from prison. Back then, a prison wasn't like today's American version with its televisions, workout equipment, athletic teams, correspondence courses for college degrees, and "prisoner rights." Paul's prison was probably a rat-infested dungeon—dark, dank, and dirty.

Yet he was accustomed to adversity. In fact, from the time he met Jesus on the Damascus Road, circumstances were against him. He was hunted, persecuted, and run out of town. Nevertheless, Paul seldom prayed to change his circumstances. More often, he called for prayer that would change him. He needed wisdom (see Colossians 4:2-6), strength (see 2 Corinthians 1:8-11), and for God's Word to be glorified (see 2 Thessalonians 3:1). He believed the gospel could be furthered *through* his circumstances (see Philippians 1:12-14), not in spite of them. Now that's contentment!

CHAPTER 11

A Surrendered Heart

When I hit age forty, I quit working for a pastor to pursue a sales job. That step took me well out of my comfort zone, but it made sense. After all, I had always loved home décor. When the manufacturer's representative job opened in our local gift industry, I had to jump at the chance.

Once hired, I traveled to all the retail businesses in my territory. Showing my catalogs and samples was *such fun*. The new job turned out to be a perfect occupation for someone who loves people as much as I do and who loves country décor like pine furniture, grapevine wreaths, quilts, and folk art.

From the first day on the job, I was hooked — even though business was slow in the beginning. Within a short time, the prosperity of the 1980s hit, and country was the hottest ticket in most gift stores.

There was some training on the ins and outs of selling, but basically I was on my own. At first I was nervous. Soon I realized that the only drawback to this job was getting paid on time. Each month, no matter how high my sales were, one of the people I was selling for seemed to have a lot of excuses for paying me late or for cutting a check for less than what was due: computer glitches, mail glitches. . . . You name the excuse; I heard them all — more excuses than Sears has catalogs. Why did I stick around? I loved what I was doing. Plus those checks were occasionally on time, and some of them were sizable. My husband supported us, so I wasn't dependent on the income. It was more "overflow" than anything. And I liked having a little extra spending money of my own.

Then the recession hit, and businesses began to close. Those that didn't, scaled back in buying inventory. To make matters worse, my commission checks from this one person began to bounce. They were small, and yet they bounced. Nearly every month.

By now, the excuses were laughable. I would eventually get some of my money, but never without a hassle. Just as the sales representatives prepared to revolt, a motivational trainer was brought in to "motivate" us to "sell, sell, sell." This trainer's approach was stale and phony. Worse yet, as we listened to her, we seethed in anger, thinking, *If you just paid us what is owed us, we'd sell plenty.*

Nonetheless, I stayed on because I loved the familiar. During the past seven years, I had enjoyed working with the same team of gals. I also loved the lines I was representing. I just didn't want to leave the coziness of this comfort zone.

Being quiet and soft-spoken is not my style. So when the so-called "sales motivational expert" asked how I planned on improving my sales over the ensuing months, I said, "Well, I haven't given much thought to that goal. I'm still waiting to be paid for sales I've made over the last several years! Why should I spin my wheels selling when it's such a hassle just getting paid?" It seemed logical, but not to my boss. Within a few days, I was asked to leave.

"Oh, I'll leave all right, but not without a fight," I threatened. "You'd better buckle up, because I plan on hiring an attorney and suing you for every penny you have *not paid* me for the last seven years. You haven't heard the last from me!" I snarled with taut lips.

I *vowed* to get revenge. I knew all the Scriptures about vengeance being the Lord's, but I rationalized my anger as *righteous.* I believed I was entitled not only to my pay, but to my anger. I was so frustrated and upset over the situation that I cried all the way home.

"How could this happen to me!" I seethed. I had worked so hard, and I had been naïve and too trusting. Now I thought I'd been forced to leave something I loved so much, and I felt like a victim. I decided to hire a lawyer, a move my sweet husband counseled against.

"Judy, it's not worth it. Revenge is God's business," he reminded. "Let it go!"

I would not. I felt suing was the right thing to do. I felt my money had been withheld from me, and the last thing I wanted to do was let *anyone* get away with that.

I should have listened to my husband, but he didn't press the issue. I think he knew I'd find out in time what a poor decision I was making. I retained an attorney to begin the process of recovering thousands of dollars that I thought were rightly mine.

"Just you wait, just you wait," I hissed while plotting out the devastation that would soon enter this person's life. I rubbed my hands together like a crazed villain and pictured my "enemy" walking the streets in a tattered quilt, homeless.

My biggest struggle, though, wasn't the money. It was leaving the work I loved so much. I worked great hours, with great people, and I had great fun doing it! Now what? I began sinking into a depression. My husband knew how much it bothered me, because I didn't talk much to him. That in itself was grounds to call the paramedics.

Meanwhile, revenge was on my mind twenty-four hours a day. It became my favorite pastime. I plotted, planned, and hoped somehow total failure would be the outcome for this person. I saw myself standing in front of the vacant showroom reveling. *"Ah ha, you creep,"* I imagined saying. *"I'm so glad you went under!"*

However, during the litigation process I got phone calls from several store owners, ones who had become my friends over the years. They were appalled at what I said had happened and, one by one, they began recommending other manufacturers.

Within weeks I had secured enough leads to start my own business. In this new situation, I didn't have to split my commission rate with anyone. Better yet, within three and a half months, I nearly tripled my income.

A year later, I was networking across the country with other reps and building a portfolio of wonderful companies to represent. I got paid on time, and the checks didn't bounce. I didn't have the aggravation of hearing excuses each month, and I was entirely self-employed. It was amazing! Before I got fired, it had never dawned on me to start my *own* business.

It also didn't occur to me that the Lord had led me out of less-than-ideal circumstances into a far more rewarding job. What may have been meant for evil, God meant for good. He was working out a plan to change both my circumstances *and* me.

The only lingering negative involved the pending lawsuit. The attorney sent letters that read: "Mrs. Hampton, if you don't suspend this lawsuit, we will be forced to sue you for defamation of character."

Excuse me? The claim seemed preposterous. This person had no character, I thought, and probably no money. Otherwise the attorney wouldn't continue trying to frighten me into dropping the suit.

I wrestled over my options. Revenge wasn't as thrilling as I had hoped it would be. Plus I regretted ever launching the suit. This action went against the wishes of my husband and the wishes of my God (see 1 Corinthians 6:1-7).

So one morning after a fretful night's sleep, I decided to let it go. Orvey had pointed out that it was God's money, not mine, and that God was in control of these circumstances. Of course. I was not at the mercy of some person. If God thought I needed that money, I'd have it.

"Drop the suit!" I said to my attorney shortly thereafter. What a relief! What a blessed relief. I had let it go. For the first time in months, I felt peace.

Yet throughout this trial I regret that I didn't look like Jesus. I didn't act like Jesus. I didn't love like Jesus. I didn't trust like Jesus. I looked pitiful, like every other vengeful person in this sin-sick, sue-happy world. Why? Because I was living in the sin of unbelief I didn't believe God was in control.

Intellectually, most Christians seem to accept this concept—that God is in control—until circumstances get rocky. At that point, we naturally seek to change our circumstances. It seems like the best way to find true happiness and contentment. I am learning, though, that this isn't the way God works. God wants to change *me,* and He uses my *circumstances* to do it. He is the Potter; we are the clay (see Isaiah 64:8).

What were the circumstances that prompted you to give your life to the Savior? What drew you to Him? Was your life a mess? Were you discouraged and anxiety-ridden? I have asked myself those questions. And I honestly wonder if it hadn't been for what I used to call "terrible" circumstances, would I have ever surrendered my life to Him? If life had turned out like I had planned, would I have rejected the gospel?

In my life, troubling circumstances ultimately helped me find contentment in God. For instance, my teenage marriage and misery brought me to the Savior. Moving away from friends forced me to depend on God for satisfaction. Unemployment forced us to depend on God for our every need according to His riches, not ours. We learned firsthand that He is the Great Provider. Much later, our broken hearts led us to surrender our son.

But in God's presence, we found peace *before* the circumstances changed. This is what Jesus came to give us, peace in the midst of pain, no matter what the circumstances. This is what vertical living is all about. Unfortunately, our tendency is toward horizontal living. We look for peace in people, places, and things.

How easy it is to slip into horizontal living. For instance, have you ever bought a brand-new car right off the showroom floor? If so, you'll remember that wonderfully distinctive smell that says, "I'm new and I've never been used, abused, or scratched." Yeah, *this* is going to do it for me.

When I drive that new car, I feel great because the circumstances are ideal—I don't have reason to worry about a thing. For instance,

I'm confident that the oil doesn't need to be changed and the fan belts aren't worn. No need to fret about the tires either. It's the greatest feeling. What really bums me out, though, is how short-lived that smell is. I've gone into debt for a smell! Then, within a few weeks, it's gone.

It must bother others as much as it does me, because now many car-wash operations offer an air freshener called "New Car Smell." Spray it inside the car and bingo! You feel good again. That's what horizontal living is—a cheap, temporary substitute for the real thing.

The real thing is vertical living. It's an inside job the Holy Spirit produces in people with surrendered hearts.

Recently, a young woman at one of my weekend conferences told me her story of vertical living. Cheryl and her husband had been married only one year when he had a massive stroke, which left him a quadriplegic and unable to speak. He was thirty-one years old. In one brief moment, the entire course of their lives was changed. Faced with a lifetime of communicating only through eye contact and needing long-term care assistance, they began a new way of living.

They moved in with her parents, and she went to work. Nurses met his needs during the day. She took care of him at night. After one year, this lifestyle overwhelmed Cheryl. So, in a state of utter frustration and discouragement, she left the house to have a good cry.

"I can't do this, Lord," she sobbed. "I just can't do it. I don't feel like living like this. What about me? What about my dreams? What about my expectations? This is too painful, and I don't want to handle it one more day."

Then, after a few moments, the Spirit of the Lord spoke to her heavy heart. It was unmistakable: "Cheryl, when I told my children to love others, I never told them that they could do it in their own power. I said I would provide My strength and love *through* them. When you are weak, I am strong. You must let go."

Suddenly, Cheryl saw her life from a different perspective. As she walked home, she finally embraced vertical living. Opening the door of her home, she felt as though a warm liquid were filling the inside of her body. She entered her husband's room and was instantly aware of a new love for him that she had never felt.

That happened fifteen years ago. Today she says they have a beautiful marriage—a love that defies explanation. It has nothing to do with their circumstances, because their circumstances never changed. He is still a quadriplegic, although he can move three fingers on his left hand, which allows him to use a computer. He still cannot speak but, according to Cheryl, these have been the sweetest years of her life. Why?

She learned the secret. And what was it? A *surrendered* heart. A heart surrendered to God and filled with the fruit of the Spirit—love, joy, peace, patience, kindness, goodness, faithfulness, gentleness, and self-control (see Galatians 5:22-23). Isn't that what we're all searching for?

Do you want in on the deal?

Begin by building an altar, one at the feet of Jesus. And on that altar, surrender *everything* . . . dreams, idols, entitlements, and expectations. Just let them go. Now you can start living *above* the circumstances, not under them.

Bible Study

The following Bible studies can be used by individuals or groups. They are designed to help you go deeper into the subject matter of each chapter.

Chapter 1

Read chapter 1: Prince Charming in a Football Helmet.

Our Viewpoint: I had a plan for my life, and it didn't turn out the way I planned. I have made one mistake after another, and it seems I've ruined any chance for happiness.

1. What are the things in your life that have not lived up to your dreams?

2. Where did these expectations come from? Fairy tales, romance novels, movies, newspapers, magazines, family or friends? Be kind, but be specific.

3. Read Ephesians 2:1-3.

   a. What is the spiritual condition of someone who does not know Jesus Christ? What is your spiritual condition?

b. Sin will take you further than you ever wanted to go, cost you more than you ever wanted to pay, and stay with you longer than you ever wanted it to stay. Without Christ, we are slaves to sin. Yet we are surprised by our wrong choices. Why?

c. What consequences have you had to live with because of your poor choices?

d. Have you ever thought, *I've ruined my life?* If so, why?

4. According to Ephesians 2:1-3, what power rules the life of someone who is not a Christian?

5. Is it any wonder we run to people, places, and "circumstances" instead of to God in order to try to find meaning and purpose for life? In the past, where have you run?

6. Most of us believe that changing our circumstances will bring us the happiness we are searching for. What do *you* think will bring you happiness?

❧ *God's Viewpoint:* The circumstances and choices you have made simply reveal your spiritual condition. The problem is not your circumstances. The problem is, you do not know Me. No person, place, or thing can satisfy the longings of your heart. Only I can do that (see Psalm 90:14).

Chapter 2

Read chapter 2: Perfect Marriages and Other Fairy Tales.

Our Viewpoint: A happy marriage is something I've dreamed about most of my life as the fulfillment of all my expectations. But it hasn't worked out the way I planned. Maybe I married the wrong person.

1. Read Genesis 3:13-19.

    a. Is it possible to have a perfect marriage? Why or why not?

    b. List some of the areas of perfection you are still seeking in your marriage.

    c. Have you struggled with pointing out imperfections in your spouse?

    d. What has been the result?

2. Satan's goal was to convince Adam and Eve to take their eyes off God and put them on themselves.

a. Do you see him doing this in marriages today? How?

b. Do you see him doing this in *your* marriage? How?

3. Read Galatians 5:19-21.

   a. Which "deeds of the flesh" seem prevalent in your marriage? Where do they come from?

   b. How have these deeds affected your marriage?

   c. What must take place in your life before your marriage can change?

4. Read 1 Corinthians 13.

   a. According to this chapter, what is love?

b. Is this the same kind of love we read about in Galatians 5:22?

c. According to 1 John 4:19, how do we obtain this kind of love?

d. If the fruit of His Spirit was evident in your life, what changes would take place in your marriage?

5. Read Ephesians 5:22-29. Because God is a God of order, He gives some practical instruction about the roles of husbands and wives.

a. In what way is the Holy Spirit speaking to you about your role in your marriage?

b. Are you arguing with God's plan? If so, write out some of your arguments so you can hear how they sound.

c. When two kings try to rule the same kingdom, what are the results?

6. In Colossians 3:17 we read, "And whatever you do in word or deed, do all in the name of the Lord Jesus." If that were your motivation, how would it affect your marriage?

7. It has been said that in order for life to come back into a marriage, one or both partners must be willing to "die to self" and to live for Christ.

   a. Name some specific ways you can begin "dying to self."

   b. Explain how these could change your marriage.

   c. Read Psalm 86:11-13. After reading it, use it as your prayer and make a commitment to walk in truth with an undivided heart.

✎ *God's Viewpoint:* Perfect love and genuine meaning for life come from Me (see John 14:6). If you will allow Me to change you, I will change your marriage.

Chapter 3

Read chapter 3: The Visit.

Our Viewpoint: What kind of supernatural love is this? I can't comprehend it. I've made such a mess out of my life. Let me clean up my life first, God. Let me do something to at least help pay the cost of my redemption.

1. Read 1 Timothy 1:15-16 and Romans 5:6-8.

    a. Can you think of anyone who would die for you?

    b. Would this kind of love have conditions? Explain.

2. Read John 6:44.

    a. How was God drawing you to Himself before you met Him? How is He drawing you now?

    b. Describe your response to His drawing.

3. Jesus said, "I am the way, and the truth, and the life; no one comes to the Father, but through Me" (John 14:6).

a. Explain what it was like the day you believed that Jesus was the only way to God.

b. Read Ephesians 1:13. What happened the day you believed?

4. Read 2 Corinthians 5:17. Part of this verse says, "Old things passed away; behold, new things have come."

   a. Think about this verse as it relates to your life in Christ. Do you see a time when old things passed away and you were a new person because of Christ?

   b. What are some of the "new things" in your life?

5. Read 2 Corinthians 5:21; Galatians 2:20; and Ephesians 2:8-9.

   a. Is there anything we can do to "earn" righteousness?

   b. Is there something *more* we must do to add to our salvation? If so, what? (See Galatians 3:1-3.)

6. Read 2 Corinthians 13:5. Have you ever tested your own heart to make certain that you have received Jesus Christ as your Lord and Savior? Do you believe the following?

> ✂ Jesus Christ is the Son of God, God in human flesh (see John 1:1,14).

> ✂ He surrendered His perfect, sinless life upon the cross to pay for the sins of the world, including mine (see Hebrews 9:11-14).

> ✂ On the third day He rose from the dead (see Acts 10:40).

> ✂ And now He is seated at the right hand of God and ever lives to make intercession for me (see Hebrews 7:25; Luke 22:69).

7. Have you ever received the gift of salvation? If so, describe how it happened.

✂ *God's Viewpoint:* "But as many as received Him, to them He gave the right to become children of God, even to those who believe in His name, who were born not of blood, nor of the will of the flesh, nor of the will of man, but of God" (John 1:12-13).

Chapter 4

Read chapter 4: Beyond the Altar.

Our Viewpoint: I'm glad I'm now a Christian, but I am still anxious to go on with the plans I have for my life. Surely those are Your plans, aren't they, Lord?

1. Read Philippians 1:6.

    a. How does this verse make you feel?

    b. What are some of the practical ways this verse gives you hope for your future?

2. Read Ephesians 2:10 and James 1:22.

    a. What are some of the ways we can walk in good works by being doers of the Word?

    b. Are you trying to live your life in such a way that you are a doer of the Word, or are you living your life simply for your own to-do list? Are there some changes that need to take place in your life? If so, what?

3. Read Ephesians 5:15-17.

  a. How do you think a Christian can walk wisely and know God's will?

  b. What happens when we are not in the Word and trying to seek His will?

  c. How do you spend most of your days? How do you spend most of your spare time?

  d. Do you know God's purpose and plan for your life? What do you think it is?

  e. Memorize Proverbs 9:10. After memorizing it, ask the Lord to make His will your will, and to help you leave the details to Him.

4. Read Ephesians 4:11-13 and 1 Peter 4:10-11.

  a. What gifts has God given you to use for His service?

b. What are you doing with your gifts?

c. What is your motivation for serving the Lord?

d. What changes need to be made in your life so you can begin serving the Lord more faithfully?

5. As young Christians, we still think about self most of the time. We live to be served, not to serve.

a. According to Mark 10:45, how did Jesus live His life?

b. As a member of the family of God, we need to mature so God can use us. What are you doing on a daily basis to help yourself mature?

c. Memorize Psalm 37:4. What are the desires of your heart?

d. How would you like God to use you?

6. Read 2 Peter 3:18.

a. In what ways are you growing in the grace and knowledge of our Lord?

b. How has this growth changed your view of your circumstances?

✺ *God's Viewpoint:* "Do not be foolish, but understand what the will of the Lord is" (Ephesians 5:17). The abundant life is not found in trying to control your life. It is found in knowing My will for your life.

Chapter 5

Read chapter 5: Forgiveness or Promissory Note?

Our Viewpoint: There is no way I am going to forgive that person. Just look what that so-and-so did to me.

1. Read 1 Corinthians 13:5.

   a. What are some of the wrongs you have suffered at the hands of someone else?

   b. As you look back over that time, what feelings has it produced?

   c. How have you responded to these feelings?

   d. Read Romans 8:28. Have you ever thought about this verse in light of what someone has done to you? If God causes all things to work together for good and is in control of everything, do you think you could thank Him for allowing this (see 1 Thessalonians 5:18)? Why or why not?

e. The passage in 1 Corinthians 13 speaks of the perfect, *agape* love. For this kind of love, we need to lean on Christ. What else must we do in order to forgive someone?

2. Read Mark 11:25; Psalm 66:18; and Isaiah 59:1-2.

a. What condition must be met before our prayers are heard or answered?

b. Read Ephesians 4:32. God asks us to forgive one another just the way He has forgiven us. Are there people in your life you refuse to forgive? In light of how God has forgiven you, how do you rationalize your unforgiveness?

c. 1 John 1:9 tells us that if we confess our sins, God is faithful to forgive us and cleanse us from all unrighteousness. Is there a part of your life that feels dirty? If so, take a look at David's confession in Psalm 51. Does this psalm help you with your own confession? How?

3. Read Hebrews 12:15.

    a. Over time, what takes place in a person's life who refuses to forgive?

    b. How has this passage spoken to you specifically? Is there someone you've harbored unforgiveness toward? What has been the result?

    c. Read Romans 12:19. Most of us agree that we should not take revenge on someone. So why is it one of life's sweetest temptations?

    d. Describe a time you sought revenge on another person.

    e. What were the results?

4. Read Romans 8:1.

    a. What is one of the great benefits about being "in Christ"?

b. Read Psalm 103:10-12. What do the passage in Romans and this psalm say about God's forgiveness? How is it possible?

c. Ask yourself this question: What is so great about me that God can forgive me, and so bad about someone else that I can't forgive them? Name the person you can't forgive. Now spend some time praying for that person. After you have prayed, is it easier to forgive that person?

d. We must assume responsibility for our unforgiving spirit toward someone else. Take a moment and ask God to forgive you for your unforgiveness. Now ask Him to forgive that person through you.

5. Read Ephesians 4:1-3,32.

a. What distinction should we have as Christians?

b. Ask yourself this question: If I were to become a person who forgives others, how would it affect my life? My friendships? My marriage? My children? My witness?

c. Take a few minutes to pray for opportunities to love and forgive like Jesus.

❧ *God's Viewpoint:* "You can't get forgiveness from God, for instance, without also forgiving others. If you refuse to do your part, you cut yourself off from God's part" (Matthew 6:14, MSG).

Chapter 6

Read chapter 6: Hey, What About <u>My</u> Rights?

Our Viewpoint: It's *my* life, and *I've* got my rights. I've *earned* them. And I won't put up with other people's ill treatment!

1. In this chapter, I share a story about my husband and me painting our house. A lot of tension in that story came from me demanding my rights. Has there been a time when you demanded *your* rights? What were the circumstances? Was it with an employer? Teacher? Parent? Spouse? What was your motive? What was the outcome?

2. Comment on a time when you were publicly humiliated. How did it make you feel? Have you ever wanted to get even for that incident?

3. As Christians, we are called to be seekers of truth, not defenders of rights. Which end of that spectrum are you closest to? Have you ever manipulated certain circumstances to prove you were right when you knew God's Word said otherwise? Explain.

4. You'd think somewhere along life's path Christ would have said, "These people aren't worth redeeming. This is too degrading, too demeaning." Why do you think He chose to take on the sins of the whole world by dying on a cross? What was His motive and what was His attitude?

5. Read 1 Corinthians 2:16 and Philippians 2:5-8.

   a. What is the one thing that characterizes the mind of Christ?

   b. Why can't we be humble? Why do we want to stand on our own two feet and do things our way?

   c. If humility is one of the hallmarks of Christ's character, what does that tell you about what God values? Read Matthew 5:1-11. What is first in the list of character qualities that God blesses?

d. Have you ever suffered for doing something right? Explain how it made you feel. For encouragement, read 1 Peter 2:19-23; 1 Peter 4:12-16; 1 Peter 5:10; and 2 Corinthians 1:3-5.

6. Christ stepped from heaven's glory to come down and live among us (see John 1:1,14).

   a. According to Philippians 2:7, why didn't He exalt in His position?

   b. Christ emptied Himself of all His rights and entitlements. He was born in a stable to a poor family. He spent His youth in a carpenter's shop. Yet God's plan to redeem us was accomplished by Christ's humiliation. Comment on or write about a time when you sacrificed your rights for the sake of someone else.

   c. Read Philippians 2:8. Christ took on the humiliation of becoming a man, yet *we* are obsessed with elevating self. In what areas of your life do you struggle for "throne rights" (that is, lifestyle, economic status, family, work, church, friendships, and so on)?

d. Within the following Scriptures, find prescriptions for a more humble walk and jot them down.

Luke 14:11

Romans 12:1-3

2 Corinthians 12:7-10

Psalm 8:3-4

Psalm 131:1

Mark 8:34

James 4:6-10

1 Peter 5:5

Which one did the Holy Spirit use most to touch your heart?

7. Read Matthew 12:9-21; Mark 10:35-45; and Philippians 2:7.

a. Demanding our rights and relinquishing our rights are mutually exclusive. We have a choice. We can serve others or we can serve self. He must increase; we must decrease. Jesus said true greatness was serving others (see Matthew 23:11). It was also the way He lived His life (see Mark 10:45). In what areas of your life are you especially prone to exalting self at the expense of others? Write down ways this can be changed.

b. Read Mark 10:43-45. If you made a decision today to stop defending your rights and start serving others, what would the results be, especially in terms of your relationships?

8. Write out your commitment to surrender your rights, giving the Lord permission to humble you and give you a servant's heart.

✎ *God's Viewpoint:* "God is opposed to the proud, but gives grace to the humble. Humble yourselves, therefore, under the mighty hand of God, that He may exalt you at the proper time" (1 Peter 5:5-6). "I have been crucified with Christ; and it is no longer I who live, but Christ lives in me; and the life which I now live in the flesh I live by faith in the Son of God, who loved me, and delivered Himself up for me" (Galatians 2:20).

Chapter 7

Read chapter 7: Growing Up or Growing Old?

Our Viewpoint: What on earth did I ever do to deserve a trial like this? This doesn't make any sense. Why are you doing this to me, God? And why now?

1. What is the hardest trial you've ever had to face? What was your response? Do you see any benefits from that trial?

2. Read Deuteronomy 8 for God's warning about good times. What is your spiritual life like when things are going along smoothly? Do the good times move you closer to God or further away?

3. God's purpose in using trials to mold us should not catch us by surprise or leave us angry and perplexed. Yet they do. Why? Give some thought to the suffering Christ experienced and compare His response to ours when we suffer (see 1 Peter 2:18-23).

   a. Read Psalm 119:71. Do you see any purpose for the trial you are in today? What are a few statutes or decrees you've learned, as spoken of in this verse?

   b. Read Psalm 119:28. When difficulties come into your life, do you run to the Word of God for comfort, or to the world? Explain.

4. It has been said that our response to a trial is the measuring stick of our faith. It will reveal whether our trust is in our circumstances or in God, who controls the circumstances. Who or what are you trusting in for the trial you are presently experiencing?

5. What is the trial you are going through revealing about your spiritual maturity?

6. Read the following verses and jot down how God wants us to respond to trials.

a. James 1:2-4

b. Romans 5:3-5

c. Job 2:10

d. Hebrews 12:1-11

7. Spiritual maturity comes from feeding on God's Word daily. It changes our view of life. How much time do you spend in the Word of God—daily, weekly, or monthly?

8. Read the following Scriptures and comment on why we must be in the Word of God.

a. Romans 10:17

b. Matthew 4:1-11

c. Romans 2:13

If you have never made a commitment to study God's Word every day, will you take a few minutes and make that commitment now?

✤ *God's Viewpoint:* "Therefore we do not lose heart, but though our outer man is decaying, yet our inner man is being renewed day by day. For momentary, light affliction is producing for us an eternal weight of glory far beyond all comparison, while we look not at the things which are seen, but at the things which are not seen; for the things which are seen are temporal, but the things which are not seen are eternal" (2 Corinthians 4:16-18).

Chapter 8

Read chapter 8: Out of the Nursery.

Our Viewpoint: I bargained for the comfy, cozy, hothouse Christian life. I want what Jesus has to offer, but I want what the world has to offer, too. My situation is less than ideal. Okay, I'm falling apart. What are You up to, God? Do something, for heaven's sake!

1. When you gave your life to Christ, what were your expectations of what the Christian life was going to be? How have your experiences been different from your expectations?

2. Describe your idea of a comfort zone. Consider some of the greatest people in the Bible, like Noah, Moses, Abraham, Peter, and Paul. Did they live in comfort zones? When? When didn't they?

3. Intellectually, most Christians accept the concept that God is in control of all of their circumstances. But when circumstances are less than ideal, few of us accept it experientially. Can you explain why? Do you think it is because we really don't *know* God's attributes?

4. Satan is the father of lies (see John 8:44) and the deceiver (see Revelation 12:9). And he knows we are most vulnerable to being deceived when we are children. That's what Paul tells us, too: "We are no longer to be children, tossed here and there by waves, and carried about by every wind of doctrine, by the trickery of men, by craftiness in deceitful scheming; but speaking the truth in love, we are to grow up in all aspects into Him" (Ephesians 4:14-15).

a. Think of a time you chose to believe a lie instead of the truth. What was your response: fear or faith?

b. How can we know that our thoughts and choices are based on truth?

c. Memorize Psalm 119:9,11: "How can a young man keep his way pure? By keeping it according to Thy word. . . . Thy word I have treasured in my heart, that I may not sin against Thee." What images does the word "treasured" call to mind? How is "treasure" different from "memorize"?

5. Read Romans 8:28.

   a. Do you believe God has a plan for your life? Do you believe He is in control? Where can you find His plan? What role do His Word, prayer, godly counsel, and circumstances have in discovering His plan, if any? Find Scriptures to support your answers.

   b. If God is not in control, who is? On what do you base your opinion?

6. Read Romans 8:29.

   a. Do you think trials are God's way of molding us into the image of His Son? Why or why not?

   b. If you were to be led by the Spirit of God instead of your circumstances, what do you think that peace would look like to others around you? Be specific.

c. Jesus Christ wants us to look at circumstances from a divine viewpoint instead of a human viewpoint. If you did that, how would it change your response to a trial?

d. Pick a specific trial, either one you're in now or one from your past. Describe how a divine viewpoint changed or could change you and the people around you.

7. Consider this: Christianity looks beyond the circumstances to God, who is in control of everything, working out His will.

a. Have you ever considered that God loves you, that He has a plan for your life, and that it is through *all* your circumstances that He accomplishes His will? Explain how that makes you feel.

b. Is there anything more freeing than unloading all your burdens on the only One who can bear them, working them all together for good so that He gets the glory and you get the peace? Why would someone refuse such an offer?

8. In the story about my husband's unemployment, God used that circumstance to draw Orvey to His Word and to mature his faith. As a result, his view of his circumstances changed. He put his trust in the Lord, not in a job. Difficult circumstances are doorways of opportunity over whose thresholds we are taken from infancy to maturity. Comment on or write about a specific time when God used difficult circumstances to help you mature.

Acknowledge before God that you are surrendering every area of your life today. Ask Him to forgive you for being rebellious and trying to live your life independent of Him. Ask Him to give you His peace in the midst of your circumstances. Thank Him for what He is going to do. This is what Christianity is all about—not what we can do for God, but what a sovereign God does in us and through us. Amen!

✎ *God's Viewpoint:* "For it is God who is at work in you, both to will and to work for His good pleasure" (Philippians 2:13). "God causes all things to work together for good to those who love God, to those who are called according to His purpose" (Romans 8:28). "Commit your way to the Lord, trust also in Him, and He will do it" (Psalm 37:5). Change your viewpoint from one that is temporal (human) to one that is eternal (divine), and it will change your attitude. Reflecting on My Word will help bring about that change.

Chapter 9

Read chapter 9: Victory or Valium?

Our Viewpoint: My circumstances are hopeless. I can't do anything *but* worry. A person would have to be out of touch with reality if they didn't worry at a time like this. There is no way I can have peace in the midst of this situation.

1. Make a list of the things you worry about the most. Rank them in order from greatest to least.

2. Do you remember the day you were saved? You made a decision by faith to trust God for all eternity, saving you from hell. If you can trust Him for salvation, is there anything you can't trust Him for?

3. Read Hebrews 11:6, focusing on the part of the verse that says, "Without faith it is impossible to please Him." We are to walk by faith, not by our human understanding (see Proverbs 3:5-6) nor by our feelings about our circumstances (see Psalm 46).

   a. When you are caught up in anxiety, who or what do you trust in?

   b. In what ways has the object of your trust proved unworthy of your trust?

c. How do fear and hopelessness get a stronghold in our lives? (A stronghold is anything in our lives that we've never surrendered to Christ.)

d. What are some examples of when you've run to the world's wisdom for a solution to your worries? What was the result?

e. Usually, the world's wisdom is so destructive because it's so deceptive. It's deceptive because usually some portion of it is true. In the examples you picked, explain what part was true and what part was a lie.

4. Read 2 Timothy 1:7.

   a. Where do fear and worry come from?

   b. Do you think they are a spiritual problem? Why or why not?

   c. God said, "Fear not," many times. Fear is the opposite of what?

d. Read Matthew 6:25-33. What did Jesus have to say in this passage about worrying? What is the significance that He used one example from the sky and one from the earth?

5. Read Philippians 4:6-7.

a. What is your first response to a crisis? What emotions do you experience, and what do those emotions lead you to do?

b. What are your thoughts about worry being a sin? What is the root cause of worry?

c. Worry means you are being mastered by your circumstances. Worry *is* a sin. But it's a sin for which God has a marvelous solution. Confession. He says in 1 John 1:9 that He'll be faithful to forgive us. Run to the Father's arms, won't you? And in His arms confess your worry, asking Him to forgive you. How do you feel now?

6. Read Daniel 4:34-35. God rules over all. Nothing happens without His permission.

   a. Because God is in control of all our circumstances, do you believe the predicament you are in today is part of His plan?

   b. Do you think He can be trusted to handle your situation, working it together for good? If not, who do you think can?

7. Most of the apostle Paul's life was lived in the midst of difficult circumstances (see 2 Corinthians 11:22-28). Some were life-threatening (see Acts 27). Yet he knew the answer to worry (see Philippians 4:6-7).

   a. When do you pray? How often? Under what circumstances?

   b. After you've prayed, how do you generally feel—more peaceful or more anxious? Explain your answer.

   c. Being thankful in all circumstances is God's will for our lives (see 1 Thessalonians 5:18). Why? Because our lives are in His hands. Tomorrow does not belong to us; it belongs to Him. Take time to thank God now for whatever you are going through. Thank Him for allowing it, and thank Him for what He is going to do through it.

d. Make a list of the things you need to start praying for, putting them in order of God's priorities for your life.

e. Take that list of priorities and pray through it every day for a week to start with, and see how it affects you. By thanking God in these circumstances, in what ways would it change your life?

8. Paul tells us something will happen to our emotions when we pray about everything.

a. What happens, according to Philippians 4:6-7?

b. Is this an emotion that the world can provide? In what way, if any, and to what measure?

c. How can we have peace in the midst of pain? According to John 14:27, where does such peace come from?

d. When we have a totally surrendered heart in the midst of difficult circumstances, who have we given control over to?

e. The reality of Christ giving peace in the midst of horrible circumstances is what Christianity is all about. Do you think submitting to God's will is a one-time commitment or a lifelong one? Why?

Make a commitment today to get serious about developing a powerful prayer life. Get organized, get started, and get excited about what God is going to do in your life.

✣ *God's Viewpoint:* "God is our refuge and strength, a very present help in trouble" (Psalm 46:1). "Cast your burden upon the LORD, and He will sustain you; He will never allow the righteous to be shaken" (Psalm 55:22). "casting all your anxiety upon Him, because He cares for you" (1 Peter 5:7).

Chapter 10

Read chapter 10: Contentment in a Crowded Heart.

Our Viewpoint: If I could just have this one thing, then I know I could be contented.

1. Read Hebrews 13:5-6.

   a. Have you ever thought that money was the solution to your discontent? Give a specific example and explain why you thought that.

   b. God talks a lot about money in His Word. Read 1 Chronicles 29:12. Where do you think our money comes from? Read Psalm 24:1. Do you think the money you have earned comes primarily from your hard work, your education, your talent, or your connections?

   c. Read 1 Timothy 6:10. According to this verse, is money evil? Why do you think that money casts such a seductive spell over us?

   d. Read Matthew 6:21. There are specific indicators that warn us if we are loving money more than God. Name some of them.

2. One of the problems with having great wealth is acquiring more, protecting what we have, flaunting it, and even sinning with it.

   a. Read the following Scriptures and write down how money can distract us from doing what God asks us to do.

      Matthew 16:24-26

      Matthew 22:35-39

      Luke 12:13-21

      Luke 16:19-31

   b. Read Ecclesiastes 5:10. Is there ever enough money? Why?

3. Most of us have struggled with the idea that money brings contentment. If this is true, how is it possible for Christians who are poor, even living in the Third World, to obtain it?

   a. Read the story again about my father-in-law (starting on page 107). Why does he have contentment?

b. Read Philippians 4:12. Are we born with contentment?

c. Read Philippians 4:13. Contextually, what are "all things" or "everything"? What part did God play in giving Paul the confidence he displayed in this verse? Is contentment available to all or just to Christians?

4. Contentment is a gift from God that comes through Christ, who imparts it to us through the Holy Spirit.

a. Read John 15:4-5. If contentment is a gift, is it a conditional or unconditional gift? In other words, do you have to do something (conditional) to get this gift, or does it come to us automatically (unconditional) as one of the benefits of becoming a Christian?

b. The mind is like a computer hard drive. It has only so much room to store data. How much space in your hard drive is taken up with self? How much of it is taken up with God?

5. Read 1 Timothy 6:6.

    a. What do you think this verse means?

    b. Contentment is available to every child of God. Name some Christians you know who are truly contented. What is the common thread that runs through all of their lives?

    c. Read Philippians 4:19. Take a few moments to reflect on it. One way to do this is to read the verse as many times as there are words in it, emphasizing a different word each time you read it. Jot down some of your insights.

6. Read Psalm 63:1-5.

    a. What should motivate us in our daily life?

    b. What motivates *you?*

7. Read Romans 12:1-2.

a. If we have our eyes fixed on the world instead of on God, what are the results?

b. The apostle Paul tells us in 2 Corinthians 4:16-18 that our view of life will determine our contentment. Read these verses and explain what he meant.

c. Where was Paul when he wrote the book of Philippians (see Acts 16:16-34)? What was Paul's response to his circumstances? How did these circumstances turn out for the greater progress of the gospel?

d. Write down some harsh circumstances you have endured in which something similar happened to you and through you.

8. Contentment is an "inside job," produced by the indwelling of God's Holy Spirit. It has nothing to do with our circumstances. It has everything to do with Jesus.

a. Take time to consider what is robbing you of contentment. What is it? In what ways is it robbing you? If this robbing goes on too long, what do you think will be the results?

b. The truly rich person is the one who needs nothing because he is content in every circumstance. Knowing that God has held Himself responsible for providing for our needs is liberating (see Matthew 6:8-13,25-34; Philippians 4:19). List a few of your needs below. Then use the list as a prayer list and thank Him for each one.

God's Viewpoint: "Godliness actually is a means of great gain, when accompanied by contentment. For we have brought nothing into the world, so we cannot take anything out of it either. And if we have food and covering, with these we shall be content" (1 Timothy 6:6-8).

Chapter 11

Read chapter 11: A Surrendered Heart.

Our Viewpoint: Boy, am I under the circumstances. And is it ever miserable down here. Absolutely miserable. I wonder what I can do to change these circumstances so I can be happy?

1. What circumstances are you presently under? Are they making you miserable or is the pressure from them molding you into a more Christlike person?

2. Most of us have an idea of what we would like to get out of life. What used to be your idea? Did it come true? Why or why not?

3. How many of your ideas were based on satisfying self? On pleasing others? Who in particular?

4. What circumstances, positive or negative, came along that changed your idea of what you would like to get out of life?

5. Read Isaiah 64:8 and Jeremiah 18:1-6.

   a. Have you ever looked at your life as a lump of clay? In these verses, we see that God wants to change us from a useless lump of clay to a vessel that brings glory to Him. How do you see Him doing that in your life?

   b. What circumstances has God used to change you?

   c. Think about the circumstances surrounding the day you met Jesus. Looking back, what would you change about them?

6. Read Psalm 40:2-3.

   a. Share a story of an especially difficult time when God rescued you and used that circumstance to bring Him glory.

   b. Read Philippians 1:12. List some ways God has used your circumstances to further the gospel.

c. Read 1 Thessalonians 5:16-18. Why is God telling us to rejoice always, pray continually, and thank Him in all circumstances?

7. The apostle Peter wrote, "His divine power has granted to us everything pertaining to life and godliness, through the true knowledge of Him who called us by His own glory and excellence" (2 Peter 1:3).

a. This verse speaks of the sufficiency of Jesus Christ. That means He is all we need. We don't need to add one single thing more. How do you think this truth could change your heart?

b. Jesus Christ is sufficient for our past, our present, and our future. Are you looking at your circumstances from the human viewpoint instead of from God's Word? What is your viewpoint producing—faith or fear?

c. Do you struggle with life because you cannot accept that God allows difficult circumstances? Read in the following Scriptures about difficult circumstances God allowed in other people's lives, then jot down insights into your own circumstances.

Job 1:1–2:10 (Note especially 1:12 and 2:6.)

Luke 22:31-34, 54-62

8. Our joy has nothing to do with our circumstances, it has everything to do with Christ.

   a. "The fear of man brings a snare, but he who trusts in the LORD will be exalted" (Proverbs 29:25). When we take our eyes off Jesus and onto our circumstances, it produces fear (see Matthew 14:22-30). Circumstances can keep us from being able to fix our eyes on Jesus. What else keeps us from that (see Hebrews 12:1-2)?

May I encourage you to build an altar? You know, one in the center of your heart. Will you surrender all of your circumstances, all of your dreams, all of your idols, all of your expectations—everything you hold on to? Ask God to forgive you for trying to find peace and joy through them. Then surrender them to Him. Let go. Thank Him for His grace that gives you the strength to make that decision. Now praise Him for everything you can think of.

  God's Viewpoint: "Rejoice always; pray without ceasing; in everything give thanks; for this is God's will for you in Christ Jesus" (1 Thessalonians 5:16-18).

TWO RESPONSES TO CIRCUMSTANCES

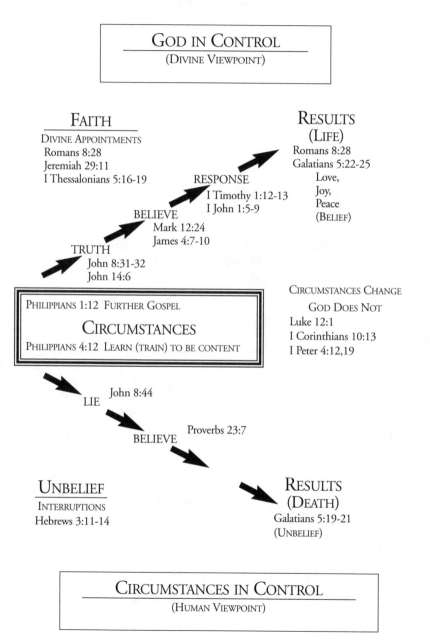

GOD IN CONTROL
(DIVINE VIEWPOINT)

FAITH
DIVINE APPOINTMENTS
Romans 8:28
Jeremiah 29:11
I Thessalonians 5:16-19

RESPONSE
I Timothy 1:12-13
I John 1:5-9

BELIEVE
Mark 12:24
James 4:7-10

TRUTH
John 8:31-32
John 14:6

RESULTS
(LIFE)
Romans 8:28
Galatians 5:22-25
Love,
Joy,
Peace
(BELIEF)

PHILIPPIANS 1:12 FURTHER GOSPEL
CIRCUMSTANCES
PHILIPPIANS 4:12 LEARN (TRAIN) TO BE CONTENT

CIRCUMSTANCES CHANGE
GOD DOES NOT
Luke 12:1
I Corinthians 10:13
I Peter 4:12,19

LIE John 8:44

BELIEVE Proverbs 23:7

UNBELIEF
INTERRUPTIONS
Hebrews 3:11-14

RESULTS
(DEATH)
Galatians 5:19-21
(UNBELIEF)

CIRCUMSTANCES IN CONTROL
(HUMAN VIEWPOINT)

Notes

Chapter 7

1. From *Shadowlands.* Spelling Film International, Los Angeles, 1993.

Chapter 8

1. George Mueller, as quoted by Mrs. Charles Cowen, *Streams in the Desert,* vol. 1 (Grand Rapids, Mich.: Zondervan, n.d.), p. 165.
2. *Streams in the Desert,* p. 238.

Chapter 9

1. Oswald Chambers, *My Utmost for His Highest* (New York: Dodd, Mead & Company, 1935), July 4, p. 186.
2. J. Vernon McGee, *Thru the Bible with J. Vernon McGee,* vol. 5 (Pasadena, Calif.: Thru the Bible Radio, 1983), p. 322.
3. Chambers, August 6, p. 201.
4. Ron Mehl, *Surprise Endings* (Sisters, Ore.: Multnomah, 1993), p. 152.

Chapter 10

1. Warren Wiersbe, *Being a Child of God* (Nashville, Tenn.: Thomas Nelson, 1996), p. 84.

A Note from the Author . . .

~

Are the circumstances in your life revealing your need to know God personally through His Son, Jesus Christ? Dear Friend, God wants to give you new life in Christ.

The Bible teaches us that God loves us. He wants us to know Him.

> For God so loved the world, that He gave His only begotten Son, that whoever believes in Him should not perish, but have eternal life. (John 3:16)

What prevents us from knowing God personally? We are sinful and separated from God, so we cannot know Him or experience His great love.

> All have sinned and fall short of the glory of God. (Romans 3:23)

Our sin leads to death and judgment.

> The wages of sin is death. (Romans 6:23)
> And inasmuch as it is appointed for men to die once and after this comes judgment. (Hebrews 9:27)

However, Jesus Christ is God's only provision for our sin. Through Him alone we can know God personally, be forgiven for our sins, and experience God's love. He died in our place on Calvary.

But God demonstrates His own love toward us, in that while we were yet sinners, Christ died for us. (Romans 5:8)

After Christ's death, He rose from the dead.

Christ died for our sins . . . He was buried . . . He was raised on the third day according to the Scriptures . . . He appeared to Cephas, then to the twelve. After that He appeared to more than five hundred." (1 Corinthians 15:3-6)

Jesus Christ is the only way to God.

Jesus said to him, "I am the way, and the truth, and the life; no one comes to the Father, but through me." (John 14:6)

It isn't enough to simply know about these things. We must make a personal decision to receive Jesus Christ and then we can know God and experience His love.

First, we need to repent of our sins. Repentance means turning from self, and independent living.

Repent therefore and return, that your sins may be wiped away, in order that times of refreshing may come from the presence of the Lord. (Acts 3:19)

We must receive Christ.

But as many as received Him, to them He gave the right to become children of God, even to those who believe in His name. (John 1:12)

We receive Christ through faith.

By grace you have been saved through faith; and that not of your-selves, it is a gift of God; not as a result of works that no one should boast. (Ephesians 2:8-9)

You can receive Christ right now by faith through prayer.

Lord Jesus, I want to know You. Thank You for dying on the cross for my sins. I open the door of my heart and receive You as my Lord and my Savior. Thank You for forgiving me of all my sins, and giving me eternal life. I surrender control of my life over to You. Please make me into the person You want me to be. Amen.

About the Author

~

Judy Hampton developed a passion for sharing the gospel shortly after her dramatic conversion at the age of twenty-five. After she and her husband moved to Southern California, she was encouraged to share her testimony with Christian Women's Clubs. Since that time, she has become a keynote speaker for conferences and retreats across the United States. Her messages are presented with practical and powerful teaching from the Word of God and energized with freshness and humor. It seems her audiences are laughing out loud one minute and wiping a tear the next.

Judy's testimony has been aired by Focus on the Family and published in several magazine articles and books. In addition to her speaking ministry, Judy is a published freelance writer and keeps very busy as a manufacturer's representative to the gift industry in Southern California, where she and her husband, Orvey, live. They have two married children, Doug and Joani, as well as five outstanding grandchildren and a very spoiled Welsh terrier!

For information on scheduling Judy to speak, please contact Speak Up Services, (888) 870-7719. Please contact Judy by e-mail at judyjudyjudy9@juno.com if you would like to share a time (or times) in your life when God orchestrated circumstances so you could share the gospel with someone. She would also like to hear about times when difficult and challenging circumstances were used by God to reveal areas in your life that were not yet surrendered to Him, and how He accomplished His will.